Pentecost, Hospitality, and Transfiguration

Toward a Spirit-inspired Vision of Social Transformation

PENTECOST, HOSPITALITY, AND TRANSFIGURATION

TOWARD A SPIRIT-INSPIRED VISION OF SOCIAL TRANSFORMATION

DANIELA C. AUGUSTINE

CPT Press
Cleveland, Tennessee

Pentecost, Hospitality, and Transfiguration
Toward a Spirit-inspired Vision of Social Transformation

Published by CPT Press
900 Walker ST NE
Cleveland, TN 37311
email: cptpress@pentecostaltheology.org
website: www.cptpress.com

Library of Congress Control Number 2012953487
ISBN-10 1935931318
ISBN-13 9781935931317

Cover: Andrei Rublyov, *The Old Testament Trinity*, icon c. 1410-1420

For Jonathan and Josiah –
Home is where you are.

TABLE OF CONTENTS

ACKNOWLEDGEMENTS

The present work originated in 2005 during my research residence as a member of the Center of Theological Inquiry in Princeton, NJ. The intellectually stimulating and scholastically prolific theological community of the Center and the weekly interactions with its members were especially helpful as many of the subthemes within the project started to take shape during this period. I am especially grateful for the encouragement and support of the Center's Director, William Storrar, who also invited me to contribute a chapter based on my research to *A World for All? Global Civil Society in Political Theory and Trinitarian Theology*, an important volume of interdisciplinary engagement with the issues of civil society that he coedited together with Peter Casarella and Paul Metzger.

I am also very grateful to the staff of the Centre for Pentecostal Theology in Cleveland, TN, where much of the research within this volume was completed during the past three years. Dr. John Christopher Thomas, the Centre's Director and Dr. Lee Roy Martin provided me with a true theological community amidst a wonderful research environment. Their ongoing constructive dialogue with my work impacted and inspired various aspects of this book's content. I am indebted to their thoughtful insights and uplifting encouragement during the writing process, as well as to their skillful work as editors of CPT Press.

I want to express my deep gratitude to Dr. Rickie Moore for his continual support of my work, as well as for his investment of time and effort in reading various portions of the text during the past two years, despite his busy schedule. Our occasional follow-up discussions have been a theological feast that has further nurtured my imagination and engagement with the themes highlighted in the book.

The moral support of Lee University's community and especially of President Paul Conn and Vice-President Carolyn Dirksen, have been an essential and invaluable aspect on the journey towards the successful completion of this project.

This work would have never been realized without the faithful and patient support of my husband and best friend, Jonathan, and our amazing son, Josiah Christopher. Together with my good friend Sabrina Evans, Jonathan has been the first reader, editor, and insightful reviewer of all my theological work.

Finally, but not least, this project may have never been conceived as an idea without the challenge of our friend, the esteemed public theologian, Professor Ronald F. Thiemann, who, while sipping coffee with me and Jonathan during a visit in Prague, casually asked the loaded question, 'What is the one book that you want to write?' During the years that followed, his thoughtful advice and guidance have been a precious gift to me that has navigated my theological research at its most important crossroads.

Since the completion of this work was spread over a number of years, revised versions of some subsections within Chapters 1, 2 and 3 have appeared in preceding publications. These include: 'Pentecost Communal Economics and the Household of God', *Journal of Pentecostal Theology* 19 (2010), pp. 119-242; 'The Empowered Church: Ecclesiological Dimensions of the Event of Pentecost', in John Christopher Thomas (ed.), *Toward a Pentecostal Ecclesiology: The Church and the Fivefold Gospel* (Cleveland, TN: CPT Press, 2010), pp. 157-80; 'Pentecost as the Church's Cosmopolitan Vision of Civil Society', in William Storrar, Peter Casarella and Paul Metzger (eds.), *A World for All? Global Civil Society in Political Theory and Trinitarian Theology* (Grand Rapids, MI: Eerdmans, 2011), pp. 197-220; 'Pentecost, Empowerment and Glossolalia', special issue on Pentecostal Ecclesiology, Veli-Matti Kärkkäinen, guest editor, *International Journal for the Study of the Christian Church* 11.4 (November 2011), pp. 288-304; and 'Pentecost and Prosperity in Eastern Europe: Between Sharing of Possessions and Accumulating Personal Wealth', in Amos Yong and Katy Attanasi (eds.), *Pentecostalism and Prosperity: The Socio-economics of Global Renewal* (New York: Pelgrave Macmillan, 2012), pp. 189-212. I am most grateful to the publishers and editors of these journals and volumes for permission to use revised portions of the texts in the present book.

My hope is that this work will be helpful to anyone studying the significance of the event of Pentecost and the beauty of divine hospitality within the process of the providential transfiguring of this world into the Kingdom of God. All buildings at Lee University are marked with an inscription – Psalm 90.17 – 'And let the favor of the Lord our God be upon us; And do confirm for us the work of our hands; Yes, confirm the work of our hands'. This is my prayer as I humbly offer this volume to its readers.

Daniela C. Augustine
Lee University
Fall 2012

CONTEXTUAL INTRODUCTION: RECOVERING SOCIO-TRANSFORMATIVE DAY-DREAMING BETWEEN THE RISE AND FALL OF EMPIRES

This is not a traditional introduction – it does not follow the conventional recipes for gently easing the readers into the content of a book while stimulating their curiosity and intellectual appetite. Rather, it offers an impressionistic depiction of the ideological context of the book's origin within the turbulent transition of Eastern Europe from Marxist socialism to neo-liberal capitalism. This introduction articulates the disillusionment of the post-communist countries as their dreams of mending the world and developing indigenous forms of democracy and socio-economic life sank within the urgently pressing realities of survival in the global market.

The philosophical density of the introduction's first section may be rather repelling to those who would prefer to engage directly with the thematic substance outlined by the book's title. For these readers, it will be beneficial to proceed to the introduction's second section or even directly to Chapter 1. For those who dare to enter the story behind the text, may they not lose sight of the hope that has motivated its substance; namely, no existing socio-political order can cement itself as the end of human history. In the words of Dimitru Staniloae, the work of God 'is bound up *par excellence* with the category of the "new": "Behold, I make all things new" (Rev. 21.5). This is the final perspective opened for us by God.'[1]

---

[1] Dimitru Staniloae, *The Experience of God: Orthodox Dogmatic Theology*, vol. 2 *The World: Creation and Deification* (Brookline, MA: Holy Cross Orthodox Press, 2005), p. 208.

This newness of life starts here and now as the Christoforming work of the Spirit makes redeemed humanity the embodiment of the very future of the world. The Spirit unfolds the cycles of history into a salvific progression towards the eschatological horizon where this world stands transfigured into the Kingdom. There the world is finally at home – in its union with God – where the Trinitarian communal life has been translated into the life of the human community.

Lost in the Cycles of History: From Hegel to Marx and … back to Hegel

As empires crumble under the saturated pressure of a providential historical moment, and their sky-lining monuments give way under the weight of structural impossibility, humanity emerges from the ruins onto a leveled geo-political terrain. While experiencing immediate relief from the lifted burden of imperial rule, people are yet somewhat disoriented by the disappearance of their navigational landmarks and search for new points of orientation. Many celebrate the recovered freedom and wide-open vacancy of the historical horizon while others lament the loss of the past with its routinized familiarity. Immediately, alternative imperial projects start competing for the newly vacant space in order to occupy it and reorganize reality into their own likeness. As brief and general as they are, these few sentences can offer a legitimate symbolic summary of twentieth-century Eastern European history.

From the story of Babel and its multiple historical metamorphoses in the Eastern European experience, the post-communist countries know that the fall of empires is also associated with a certain degree of confusion caused by the sudden eruption of the other amidst the imperial collapse. Reopened societal vents spew to the surface multiple cultural identities, long-repressed under the monolithic imperial rule. Society suddenly experiences the untranslatable polyphony of the recovered foreign speech of our neighbors, and the immediacy of their faces summons us with a demand for recognition. In the once monotonous homogeneity of shared common spaces we witness the cultural transfiguration of our neighbors into the unknown ethnic, religious, economic, and political other.

In addition to the eruption of multiple forms of sociopolitical otherness, the fall of empires creates surges of displaced and dispossessed people – emigrants, nomads, refugees searching for a shelter and means of survival within the immediate social domain. Usually, they appear as a by-product of the lifting of homogenizing imperial pressure with its comprehensive, violently-imposed peace – a process which often results in a web of local explosions of aggression and hostility against the other and the different.[2] Alternative empires, competing for peoples' loyalties, expertly utilize the escalating societal claustrophobia provoked by the recovered presence of the other. They skillfully present the tempting vision of restoring the societal homogeneity by conveniently squeezing out all otherness and reverting the social fabric to the bliss of easily manageable monochromatic ideological existence.

The eventual advent of alternative empires amidst a newly liberated *socium* is conditioned by the population's preexistent imperial consciousness inherited from the recent past. When faced with the fear of the unknown and the disorientation at the disappearance of the old, this consciousness gravitates by default to the comfortable familiarity of imperial order. The biblical narrative of Israel's post-exodus struggles with freedom illustrates this disturbing social phenomenon. Life in the presence of and covenant with the truly free (and therefore able to liberate) God, untamed and independent of imperial political agendas, demands a transformation of human consciousness as a precursor to the realization of authentic human freedom in a covenantal community. In contrast, the court deities of Pharaoh are predictable and easy to satisfy. Their domesticated tempers and passivity in the face of injustice bring a sense of convenience and political expediency. Reflecting on Israel's nostalgia for the security of the Egyptian empire amidst the travails of God's pedagogy of freedom, Walter Brueggemann states that eventually

---

[2] Robin Wright, 'The New Tribalism: Defending Human Rights in the Age of Ethnic Conflict', *Los Angelis Times*, June 08, 1993. The author reflects on the multiple locations of violence covering the globe after the end of colonialism, communism, and the Cold War. It is not accidental that the fall of communism in Eastern Europe coincided with the outburst of the war among the countries in former Yugoslavia and within what was once upon a time the USSR. (http://articles.latimes.com/1993-06-08/news/wr-788_1_human-rights).

Israel's 'gift of freedom was taken over by the yearning for order'.[3] Indeed, history displays the dialectical tension between order and freedom as the essential internal motif navigating societal development. Many philosophers, striving to construct an account of universal human history,[4] have underscored the struggle for personal and communal freedom as being civilization's fundamental historical focus. G.W.F. Hegel was the first, among those who wrote a philosophy of history, to perceive human consciousness as the dialectical outcome of its environment's social and cultural particularities – a product of its own socio-political time and space. As Fukuyama points out, the implication of Hegel's perspective is that human history must be seen not only as a succession of different civilizations, 'but most importantly as a succession of different forms of consciousness'.[5] In the words of Hegel:

> The History of the world is none other than the progress of the consciousness of Freedom; ... the Eastern nations knew only that *one* is free; the Greek and the Roman world only that *some* are free; while *we* know that *all* [humans] ... are free.[6]

For Hegel, the Judeo-Christian tradition is to be credited for introducing within the historical process of the West the true recognition of human rights and dignity, and therefore, of freedom itself. Authentic freedom is perceived as proceeding from God's creative intent and sustained in His providence by the Spirit as history's 'in-

---

[3] Walter Brueggemann, *The Prophetic Imagination* (Fortress Press, 1978), p. 40.

[4] Kant formulates the challenge of writing a Universal History of humanity in his famous work *Idea for a Universal History from a Cosmopolitan Perspective* (1784) (full text at http://marxists.org/reference/subject/ethics/kant/universalhistory.htm). He expresses the tension between freedom and order in his reference to the 'unsocial sociability' of the human being (in the Fourth Thesis of the text). Hegel and Marx both pick up this theme from Kant in developing their socio-historical dialectics. Towards the end of his account of Universal History, namely his book *The Philosophy of History* (New York: Wiley Book Co. & Colonial Press, 1960), Hegel summarizes: 'this is the point which consciousness has attained, and these are the principle phases of that form in which the principle of freedom has realized itself, for the history of the world is nothing but the development of the idea of freedom' (p. 456).

[5] Francis Fukuyama, *The End of History and the Last Man* (New York: The Free Press, 1992), p. 62.

[6] Hegel, *Philosophy of History*, p. 19.

herent vital movement'.[7] The Spirit as an agent of salvation and reconciliation[8] introduces the emancipation of human will and the transformation of consciousness into 'that of Spirit'.[9] This ultimate stage of the human being 'interpenetrated by Deity'[10] is the realization of 'infinite Freedom'. This is the fulfillment of the historical process – it is its spiritual goal. Hegel sees the freedom of will as 'the principle and substantial basis of all Right', as the agency through which humanity becomes human and, therefore, as the 'fundamental principle of Spirit'.[11]

Hegel's position on the cultural and social preconditioning of consciousness is further reflected in his discussion on the constitutional structure of the state. In his *Philosophy of Right*, the philosopher makes the following statement:

> ... the constitution of any given nation depends in general on the character and development of its self-consciousness. In its self-consciousness its subjective freedom is rooted and so, therefore, is the actuality of its constitution ... Hence every nation has a constitution appropriate to it and suitable for it.[12]

This statement reflects the idea that each government is deserved by its people since it represents a dialectical outcome of that people's particular historical stage of self-consciousness.[13]

Hegel's historical dialectic takes the form of a Socratic-like dialogue between social orders in which the societies with less internal

---

[7] Hegel, *Philosophy of History*, p. 323.

[8] Hegel, *Philosophy of History*, pp. 322-23.

[9] Hegel, *Philosophy of History*, pp. 332-33.

[10] Hegel, *Philosophy of History*, p. 333.

[11] Hegel, *Philosophy of History*, p. 443.

[12] In *Philosophy of Right* (trans. T.M. Knox; Oxford: The Clarendon Press, 1962), §274, Hegel illustrates this point through bringing as an example the constitution given by Napoleon to the Spaniards, which in spite of being 'more rational' than their previous one, was perceived by them as 'something alien, because they were not yet educated up to its level'. Karl Marx critiques this idea stating that: 'The only thing that follows from Hegel's reasoning is that a state in which the character and development of self-consciousness and the constitution contradict one another is no real state'. *Critique of Hegel's 'Philosophy of Right'* (trans. Annette Jolin and Joseph O'Malley; Cambridge: Cambridge University Press, 1970), p. 20.

[13] Shlomo Avinery, *Hegel's Theory of the Modern State* (Cambridge: Cambridge University Press, 1972), pp. 185-93.

contradictions win the debate.[14] However, he does not see the historical dialectical process as being infinite – an eternal social *perpetuum mobile*. Hegel insists that history's 'last stage' is the self-consciousness of the Western liberal state, which he believes to be free from internal contradictions associated with previous social orders. As Shlomo Avineri points out, 'it is in the modern, post-1815 world of Western Europe that Hegel sees the apex of historical development'.[15] There, he believes, freedom has found its true actualization.[16] This is the limit of Hegel's socio-political imagination that folds Christianity's vision of the good life, its ultimate concern (namely, the Kingdom of God) into the paradigm of the Western liberal state.

While Marx methodologically adopts the Hegelian dialectic in his historical materialism, he critiques Hegel's conclusion regarding humanity's historical ends. For Marx, the Western-European liberal state cannot represent the accomplishment of universal freedom, because it prioritizes (protects and defends) the freedom of a particular class in society, namely the bourgeoisie,[17] at the expense of others. It perpetuates the social conditions for accumulation of capital through exploitation of the proletariat (being the economic other). According to Marx, the presence of class struggle in society (as an internal contradiction) manifests the fact that the consciousness of the liberal state is not the ultimate horizon of the historical process and that Hegel's conclusion confirms his own idea that human consciousness (in this case Hegel's personal consciousness) is indeed a product of its own time.[18]

Marx erroneously believed that his own ideological vision of the end of history represents a radical discontinuity with the capitalist liberal state. He described this vision's final stage as the achievement of a classless society which will lead to the depolitization of

---

[14] Fukuyama, *The End of History*, p. 61.

[15] Avineri, *Hegel's Theory of the Modern State*, p. 235.

[16] Hegel, *The Philosophy of History*, p. 442.

[17] Karl Marx and Friedrich Engels, *The Communist Manifesto* (New York: Washington Squire Press, 1964), p. 84.

[18] Karl Marx, *Critique of Hegel's Philosophy of Right* (Cambridge: Cambridge University Press, 1970). Marx saw Hegel as an apologist of the bourgeoisie, trying to prove the divinely appointed place of the liberal capitalist state as the end of the historical process.

'public power', since 'political power, properly so called is merely the organized power of one class for oppressing another'.[19] Such an eschatological outcome, according to Marx, would make necessary the formation of 'a class that is the dissolution of all classes, a sphere of society having a universal character because of its universal suffering'.[20] For Marx, this class is the proletariat, destined to bring to fruition the 'universal emancipation of society'.[21] He envisions this socio-transformative process within global parameters as a natural consequence to the fact that 'the working men [and women] have no country'[22] – they are a trans-national economic and geo-political reality. For what it is worth, it may be argued that in the distant perspective of his nineteenth-century context, Marx foresees the homogenizing power of global capitalism, bringing world-wide 'uniformity in the mode of production and in the conditions of life corresponding thereto'.[23] He believes that the omnipresent proletariat, united in transforming revolutionary action,[24] would eventually achieve universal class supremacy. This process would lead humanity to the natural resolution of ethnic conflicts and bring the advent of global peace. In Marx's words:

> In proportion as the exploitation of one individual by another is put to an end, the exploitation of one nation by another will also be put to an end. In proportion as the antagonism between classes within the nation vanishes, the hostility of one nation to another will come to an end.[25]

While the limitations of the present work do not allow for an expounded reflection on the implications of Marx's universal eschatological vision for the current discourse on globalization, it is worth noting the fact that many contemporary neo-Marxist theorists have found in it a renewed source of energy and inspiration in articulating their critiques and predictions regarding global capital-

---

[19] Marx and Engels, *The Communist Manifesto*, p. 95
[20] Karl Marx, *Critique of Hegel's Philosophy of Right*, p. 141.
[21] Karl Marx, *Critique of Hegel's Philosophy of Right*, p. 139.
[22] Marx and Engels, *The Communist Manifesto*, p. 90.
[23] Marx and Engels, *The Communist Manifesto*, p. 90.
[24] This is the idea behind the creation of the First Proletarian International.
[25] Marx and Engels, *The Communist Manifesto*, pp. 90-91.

ism.[26] They have tried to re-envision Marxist historical ends in the cultural pluralism of the global village.

Marx's ultimate vision for humanity represents, in a sense, retrogression to its pre-Babel stage of uniformity and singularity of identity and self-consciousness. It is a vision of the evolution of human consciousness to a level of successful elimination of all its alternatives and deviations. It is an effective final dissolution of the possibility of the other. The methodology towards the accomplishment of this vision starts with the proletarian revolution – a violent discontinuity with the past conducted by the class of the future. The proletariat seizes control over the present and asserts its supremacy through the establishment of a dictatorship coercing the remodeling of society into its own likeness, thus presenting itself as the ideologically uncontested form and content of the world's future. This, in essence, however, is the replacement of one empire with another.

---

[26] For examples of such an application of Marx's theory see: Beruch Berberoglu (ed.), *Globalization and Change: The Transformation of Global Capital* (Lanham, MD: Lexington Books, 2005), esp. pp. 130-37; Alex Callinicos, *An Anti-Capitalist Manifesto* (Cambridge: Polity Press, 2003); Michael Hardt and Antonio Negri, *Empire* (Cambridge, MA: Harvard University Press, 2000); and *idem, Multitude: War and Democracy in the Age of Empire* (London: Penguin Books Ltd, 2005). Hardt and Negri recontextualize Marxist theory within the conditions of globalization through redefining the content and significance of the political categories of *proletariat* and *class struggle* as a dialectical principle of social transformation, while accommodating the pressing demands of cultural multiplicity in the global village. They offer a compelling postmodern translation of Marxist theory, in an attempt to resolve the homogenizing uniformity of its original political vision. The authors redefine the concept of empire as 'the new global form of sovereignty' of Western capitalism (*Empire*, pp. 393-413) and globalize the Marxist ideal of the proletariat as being the one destined to pull down the empire through organized class struggle and resistance by broadening it into a new postmodern sociopolitical category designated as *multitude*. The scope of the multitude stretches beyond industrial labor, incorporating the forms associated with the sector of immaterial production, which the authors emphasize as being 'hegemonic in qualitative terms' in the contemporary information age (*Multitude*, p. 109). It is a *biopolitical* category 'thus indicating that the traditional distinctions between the economic, the political, the social, and the cultural become increasingly blurred' (*Multitude*, p. 109). For Hardt and Negri, this is a key to the theoretical possibility for the multitude to 'sustain an alternative democratic society on its own' (*Multitude*, p. 357) since in it economic and political production would coincide, suggesting 'a framework for a new institutional structure of society' (*Multitude*, p. 351). This structure is embedded in the 'affective, cooperative, and communicative' relationships of social production, and their natural network as internal infrastructural logic capable of sustaining a new society (*Multitude*, p. 350).

Both Hegel and Marx insist on the non-compromising absolutism of their eschatological platforms and reject the possibility of otherness as a socio-political critique and alternative to their vision of the world's future. Yet, in fairness to Hegel we have to point out that on the margins of his 'overall closed horizon of history' there are a couple of instances in which he cautiously and hesitantly leaves a space for the unknown. These moments of permissible bending of historical patterns he associated with predictions of significant roles played in the world's future by the Slavic Eastern European nations (especially Russia), and America.[27] Yet, as Avineri indicates, it is not clear whether Hegel thought that 'the future development of Russia and America would signify new "principles" of world history or just an extension of the principles already achieved'.[28] Fukuyama supports the second interpretation and utilizes Alexandre Kojevé's view on the historical process after Hegel in support of the thesis that communism did not represent a higher stage than liberal democracy but a part of the same historical stage in search of universalizing the spread of its ideas of 'liberty and equality to all parts of the world'.[29] For him, the twentieth-century history of Eastern Europe illustrates the finality of Hegel's dialectical horizon. In 1989, according to Fukuyama, the former communist countries made the full circle back to the Western socio-political reality as the only single historical option left for humanity. This return announced the end of history. Fukuyama's triumphalist conclusion, however, is symptomatic of the ethos of empire bringing a foreclosure of societal dreaming and imagination – a foreclosure of the possibility to nurture the envisioning of alternatives beyond the boundaries of the current reality. What is left for humanity is survival through adaptation to life within the boundaries of empire.

Communism was believed to represent a further development of society through resolving its internal contradictions (namely the existence of revolutionary class struggle). Yet, its imperial rule violent-

---

[27] Hegel, *Philosophy of History*, p. 350 (on the Slavs), pp. 86-87 (on America). For more on the subject see also Avineri, *Hegel's Theory of the Modern State*, pp. 234-38.

[28] Avineri, *Hegel's Theory of the Modern State*, p. 237.

[29] Fukuyama, *The End of History*, p. 66.

ly resisted any form of ideological dissidency and repressed any expression of prophetic envisioning of an alternative future. It is ironic, however, that Eastern Europe, the location of Marxism's societal experimentation, finds itself today in a historical loop in which its future is the 'already past'.[30] This reality feels, indeed, like a cinematic drama of time-travel in which the protagonists are lost in a vicious circle of historical recycling with no exodus. If social transformation could be understood as the 'future invading the present',[31] then facing the already past as the only option of one's future represents the ultimate end of the possibility for societal change. It is the end of socio-political imagination and daydreaming.

Indeed, Eastern Europe's brief euphoria of newly recovered freedom and dreams of developing indigenous models of political and economic life were quickly quenched by the demand for an expedient adaptation to the over-night advent of Western neo-liberal capitalism. Yet, the alternative of regression into the dehumanizing, oppressive communist past was a far more dreadful prospect than accepting the socio-political accommodation of the West.

Hegel offered to the world a vision of social evolution that reaches its end in the reality of the nineteenth-century Western liberal state. Marx, on the other hand, offed a vision of a social revolution that brings about a radical discontinuity with the past – a socio-political annihilation of the very roots that have produced Hegel's world. Yet, Christianity's socio-transformative vision depicting humanity's future in the critical, world-changing otherness of the Kingdom of God, is not an outcome of an evolution or a revolution but of the Spirit's 'marvelous transfiguration'.[32] This is the vision of redemption that takes the old broken world and makes all things new. It challenges both communism and capitalism with the Christoforming communal work of the Spirit that shapes the *eschton* amidst the collapse of empires and reopens social imagination by giving dreams and visions of the age to come.

---

[30] Eastern Europe's historical cycle in the twentieth century started with capitalism, moved through Marxist socialism, and ended once again in capitalism.

[31] Alvin Toffler, *Future Shock* (New York: Bantam Books, 1972), p. 1.

[32] Nicolas Berdyaev, *Philosophy of Inequality* (Sofia: Prozorec, 1998), p. 220.

In Search of an Exodus from Empire towards a Cosmopolitan Vision of Civil Society

At its current historical location, thousands of years after Babel, humanity finds itself compressed by the omnipresence of globalization and faced once again with the demanding immediacy of the language of the other.

Among the remnants of trivialized utopias, broken societal dreams and the escalating pressure of the continual demand for re-spacing under the influx of the other, it is often difficult to maintain a hopeful and creative outlook toward the future. Our hope-depleted geopolitical terrain thirsts for prophetic imagination that reopens the horizon of socio-political dreaming and creates time and space for constructing alternative visions of the world's future – visions of its socio-transformative becoming into a place of hospitality for the other, embracing them as an integral part of human flourishing in its globalized communal form.

After all, any transition to building a viable democracy (as well as attaining social emancipation and redemption) is impossible without the other. Such a transition requires a cosmopolitan vision of an inclusive, emancipated global community. In the words of Desmond Tutu, such a vision demands a spirituality of transformation that takes seriously the wellbeing of all members of society, including that of political opponents, former oppressors, present economic exploiters, abusers, torturers, and enemies.[33] Tutu points to the spirituality needed to incarnate this covenantal moral society. Such spirituality contributes to the building of what Vaclav Havel has termed 'the moral state'[34] (outside of which democracy remains an impossible project)[35] and assures the existence of 'politics as the practice of morality'.[36] Contrary to the traditional capitalist priority

---

[33] Desmond Tutu, *The Rainbow People of God* (New York: Doubleday, 1994), esp. Chapter 6.

[34] Vaclav Havel, 'Politics, Morality and Civility', pp. 391-402 in Don E. Eberly (ed.) *The Essential Civil Society Reader: Classic Essays in the American Civil Society Debate* (Lanham, MD: Rowman & Littlefield Publishers, 2000), p. 396.

[35] Havel, 'Politics, Morality and Civility', p. 401.

[36] Havel, 'Politics, Morality and Civility', p. 397.

of economic self-interest and benefit,[37] the spirituality of transformation needed in the larger global village upholds covenantal institutions of civil society[38] by prioritizing the other as an indispensable part of a just future. This spirituality draws courage from the presence of the other and speaks the language of hope on their behalf. It involves civil responsibility for the other that in turn demands 'internal restraints',[39] that is, a form of responsible and reverent consumption committed to economic and ecological justice.[40] Persons who adopt such an attitude are characterized by the civic virtue of fasting from oneself on behalf of the fellow human and the rest of nature. As thinkers both on the left and on the right have observed, the development of this type of communal consciousness requires our personal transformation. 'We can change the world if we can change ourselves'.[41]

Civil society and any economic and socio-politically just governance are matters of moral relationships.[42] In view of that, Gertrude Himmelfarb has suggested that perhaps the contemporary global crisis of democracy and capitalist production should be viewed as being the consequence of 'the moral bankruptcy that comes with the depletion of both religious and quasi-religious moral capital'.[43]

---

[37] For a more detailed political and economic exposition on the wealth accumulating and consumption reflex of capitalism, see Alex Callinicos, *An Anti-Capitalist Manifesto* (Cambridge: Polity Press, 2003), pp. 35-39.

[38] Jonathan Sacks, *The Politics of Hope* (London: Vintage, 2000). The author describes the so-called 'third-sector institutions', those sustaining the civil society in the conditions of late capitalism. He calls the relationships they form covenantal (vs. contractual) and sees them as foundational for a just society.

Jean Bethke Elshtain also highlights the need for a 'new social covenant' in 'Democracy on Trial', in *The Essential Civil Society Reader*, pp. 101-22, esp. pp. 117-20.

[39] Sacks, *Politics of Hope*, p. 268.

[40] Timothy Gorringe, 'The Principalities and Powers: A Framework for Thinking about Globalization', in Peter Heslam (ed.), *Globalization and the Good*, (London: SPCK, 2004), pp. 79-91.

[41] Sacks, *Politics of Hope*, p. 269.

[42] Michael Woolcock, 'Getting the Social Relations Right: Toward an Integrated Theology and Theory of Development', in Peter Heslam (ed.), *Globalization and the Good* (London: SPCK, 2004), pp. 41-51, and there pp. 48-49. Also Sacks, *Politics of Hope*, p. 269.

[43] Gertrude Himmelfarb, 'The Renewal of Civil Society', in T. William Boxx and Gary M. Quinlivan (eds.), *Culture in Crisis and the Renewal of Civil Life* (Lanham, MD: Rowman and Littlefield Publishers, 1996), p. 72.

According to Himmelfarb, the central question that confronts us today is whether there are 'prospects for a moral reformation of society'.[44] This question is obviously linked to a different one – that of secularization and the development of secular politics of social salvation.[45]

The Western ideas of human rights, equality, and justice have their origins in the Judeo-Christian tradition and its capacity to nurture a covenantal communal consciousness.[46] According to Gordon Graham, the world after Darwin and Nietzsche was marked by a shift from covenantal (divinely ordained) to contractual (humanly ordered) liberalism, democracy, and guardianship of human rights.[47] If Hegel and Marx were correct in arguing that self-consciousness is a product of one's cultural and historical circumstances, then it is legitimate to ask whether democracy and human rights can be authentically sustained if the historic cultural foundation on which they have been built has lost its plausibility. Reflecting on this question, Gordon Graham suggests that Locke and the biblical prophet Habakkuk 'have more in common than do Locke and contemporary liberal democracy. They both believed that the ultimate source of moral and political authority is God'.[48]

Today many would agree that the commodification of life has distorted our view of the other, robbed us of socio-transformative dreams and trivialized the diversity of the global village, reducing the world to an exchange-value at the omnipresent free marketplace. Yet, for over 2000 years, Christianity has sustained – through the rise and fall of empires – the glorious vision of world's ultimate transfiguration into a sanctuary – a house of worship and healing for all nations bonded by the Spirit into one global covenantal community (Rev. 7.9-10). The realization of this cosmopolitan destiny demands a spirituality capable of translating the future into the present within the faith-praxis of Christ's communal Body on be-

---

44 Himmelfarb, 'The Renewal of Civil Society', p. 72.

45 Gordon Graham, *The Case Against the Democratic State* (Charlottesville, VA: Imprint Academics, 2002), pp. 64-68.

46 Max Stackhouse, 'Sources and Prospects for Human Rights Ideas: A Christian Perspective', in Jindřich Halama (ed.), *The Idea of Human Rights: Traditions and Presence* (Prague, Czech Republic: UK ETF, 2003), pp. 183-84.

47 Graham, *Case Against the Democratic State*, pp. 66-67.

48 Graham, *Case Against the Democratic State*, p. 68.

half of the world. This vision and its incarnation are the threefold work of the Holy Spirit as the giver of dreams and visions. The creator Spirit inspires prophetic speech-acts. The transformer Spirit induces change in human beings and communities towards Christ-likeness. The liberator Spirit sets us free to be and to become. All in all, the Spirit is the giver and sustainer of life and hope in the face of despair. The Holy Spirit deconstructs imperial historical ends, overwhelming them from beyond their boundaries and opening an exodus out of exile and displacement, marginalization, and suffering. The Spirit guides us ultimately towards the Cosmic Christ as the One who is the Truth that sets us free and makes us whole as human beings, as communities, and as a world. As Max Stackhouse states, Christ can renew the covenant between God and humanity while pointing souls and societies toward a New Jerusalem.[49]

The present book upholds this assurance while reflecting on the need for a prophetic re-envisioning of historical ends and a hopeful political imagination within the global context. In search of socio-transformative inspiration, it looks at the event of Pentecost as offering a rapturing vision for the cosmopolitan future of the world. This vision highlights the radical hospitality of God towards the other, incarnated in the community of faith via the agency of the Holy Spirit and forecasts the redemption of humanity's multiculturalism transfiguring the global village into the city of God.

---

[49] Max Stackhouse, 'Public Theology and Political Economy in a Global Era', in William F. Storrar and Andrew R. Morton (eds.), *Public Theology for the 21st Century* (London: T&T Clark, 2004), p. 191.

1

THE EVENT OF PENTECOST: ECCLESIOLOGICAL DIMENSIONS

Introduction

If icons are 'theology in images',[1] then the iconostasis of the Church at the Theological School of Halki holds a breathtaking visual theological library. Among its treasures is an intricate piece devoted to the Holy Trinity. It offers to the viewer a pictographic translation of the Old Testament pre-incarnational revelation of the Godhead into the New Testament dimensions of God's self-revelation through the Son and the Spirit. The upper portion of the icon narrates the story of the visitation of Abraham by the three divine guests at the oak of Mamre (Gen. 18.1-15). Since no one has seen God (Jn 1.18), this is the only visual articulation of the Trinity that is considered canonical by the Eastern Orthodox Tradition.[2] The lower portion of the icon, which serves as the New Testament witness to the Trinitarian mystery, is subdivided into a triptych, communicating three distinct events from the New Testament narrative. On the left we see the depiction of Jesus' baptism in water by John the Baptist – the public Trinitarian witness to the identity of the Son through the audio-theophany of the voice the Father, and the

[1] Leonid Ouspensky, *Theology of the Icon* (Crestwood, NY: St. Vladimir's Seminary Press, 1992), I, p. 9.

[2] Perhaps the most famous iconographic depiction of what has become known as 'The Old Testament Trinity' is Andrei Rublyov's 15th-century icon, which is pictured on the front cover of this book.

visual theophany of the Spirit descending as a dove upon the Messiah. On the right, we see the icon of the Transfiguration on Mt. Tabor as an articulation of 'the humanity of the Son, manifesting forth that deity which is common to the Father and the Spirit'.[3] This time the event outlines a private witness (before the inner-circle of disciples) of Jesus as the Christ, manifested in the divine splendor of uncreated radiance. In the center of the triptych, however, we see the icon of Pentecost – the event of the transformation of the community of faith into the Body of Christ, empowered by the Holy Spirit to do the will of the Father. This is the event in which the Church is established as the image of the Trinity on earth. No wonder the Orthodox Tradition celebrates the day of Pentecost as the festival of the Trinity.[4]

It is not accidental that the Day of Pentecost described in Luke's account of the Acts of the Apostles has been identified as the birthday of the Christian church.[5] It establishes her demarcations as the charismatic *koinonia*[6] of the ones who have received God's Word of Life and have been transformed into the living Body of Christ on earth through the agency and empowerment of the Holy Spirit. Therefore, through the Christoforming[7] work of the Spirit,

---

[3] Vladimir Lossky, *The Mystical Theology of the Eastern Church* (Crestwood, NY: St. Vladimir's Seminary Press, 1997), p. 243. It is also hard to overemphasize the centrality of the event of Pentecost within Pentecostal theological reflection. The confession of Christ as Spirit-Baptizer and the corresponding sacramental practice of speaking in tongues are one of the focal points of Pentecostal theology and spirituality. The Christocentricity of the Five-fold gospel as the distinct template of Pentecostal theological inquiry highlights this confession as essential for the Church's understanding of her identity and mission. Therefore, the event of Pentecost serves as contextual origin, dialogical anchor, and continual source of inspiration and challenge within Pentecostal theological reflection. See Martin William Mittelstadt, *Reading Luke–Acts in the Pentecostal Tradition* (Cleveland, TN: CPT Press, 2010).

[4] Vladimir Lossky, *The Mystical Theology*, p. 239.

[5] Keith Warrington, *Pentecostal Theology: A Theology of Encounter* (London: T & T Clark, 2008), p. 107.

[6] For an overview of the Pentecostal/Charismatic view of the Church as a charismatic *koinonia* see Veli-Matti Kärkkäinen, *An Introduction to Ecclesiology: Ecumenical, Historical & Global Perspectives* (Downers Grove, IL: InterVarsity Press, 2002), pp. 74-76.

[7] The term is used by Frank Macchia in *Baptized in the Spirit: A Global Pentecostal Theology* (Grand Rapids, MI: Zondervan, 2006), p. 106.

the Church becomes also an extension of the *koinonia* of the Trinity in-fleshed in the redeemed human community. As teleological creation of the Triune God, the Church exhibits the synergistic work of Christ (the eternal, incarnated Word) and the Spirit according to the will of the Father. Therefore, the work (*leitourgia*) of the Body of Christ is the work of God on earth.[8] The Trinitarian dimension of the first coming of the Son is translated into His Church, for as Christ fulfilled the will of the Father in the power of the Spirit, so does also His Body, the Church, as His continuation within the material existence of this world.

The event of Pentecost ushers on the stage of salvation history the community of faith as the *One*, *Holy*, *Catholic,* and *Apostolic* ecclesia – the anointed and empowered Body of Christ representing, in its mystical union with the Redeemer (Eph. 5.32), the eschatological fusion of heaven and earth (Eph. 1.10). This is the Body that, in the power of the Holy Spirit, continues the ministry of the resurrected Christ in this world as the living extension of His character and mission.

The marks of the Church are visibly outlined in the Pentecost narrative: The disciples are 'all together in one place' (Acts 2.1) and their unity anticipates the outpouring of the Spirit, the promise of the Father (Lk. 24.49), that reaffirms their identity in Christ as God's children. The oneness of the Church is established through her organic unity with the One Christ as being His Body on earth (Eph. 1.22-23), anointed by the Holy Spirit in accordance to the will of the Father (2 Cor. 1.21-22). As Frank Macchia points out, the unity of Pentecost is 'not abstract and absolute, but rather concrete

---

[8] The present book has its roots within the Eastern European context that has been shaped by and engraved with Eastern Orthodox theology and spirituality. Therefore, it is not accidental that the Orthodox tradition has primed the theological reflection and influenced the liturgical practices of various Pentecostal streams within this part of the world. This influence is evident also in the traditional Eastern European Pentecostal view of salvation history (including the event of Pentecost) as the work of the Trinity with all three persons simultaneously present and active in God's providential engagement with the world. For more on the Eastern Orthodox ecclesiological perspective see cf. Timothy (Bishop Kallisos) Ware, *The Orthodox Church* (New York: Penguin Books, 1997), pp. 239-63.

and pluralistic'.[9] It embraces the other in their ethnic, socio-economic, and gender diversity (Acts 2.17-18), and affirms their human dignity 'as bearers of the divine image'.[10]

The divine origin of the Church's inauguration and her identity as the Body of the resurrected Christ emphasize her holiness 'in' and 'through' her ontological and eschatological union with God. The believers are positioned 'in' and united 'with' Christ as the Holy Spirit saturates them with the divine presence (Acts 2.4) making them 'partakers (*koinonoi*) of the divine nature' (2 Pet. 1.4).

There is one flame that distributes itself as tongues of fire upon each one of the believers (Acts 2.3), giving the reader a visualization of the simultaneous oneness and catholic diversity of the Body. The catholicity of the Church is further articulated by the assertion of the presence of representatives 'from every nation under heaven' (Acts 2.5) who after the proclamation of the Good News in their native tongues (Acts 2.6-11) become constituting members of the Pentecost faith community. The catholicity of the event upholds the church's unity of sustained diversity as communal oneness that celebrates personal identity within its complex corporal beauty. Worshiping the creative Trinity as its icon on earth,[11] the church reflects God's presence among humanity as the singular sustaining principle of communal diversity in co-equality and freedom. The Trinity, as the proto-community, is the very model of this catholicity expressed in love – the identifier of the Trinitarian life and of the community of believers as authentic disciples of Christ (Jn 13.35). The catholicity of Pentecost reveals the radical hospitality of God welcoming all nations under heaven into the life of the Trinity through His self-giving in the Holy Spirit. It also simultaneously

---

[9] Frank Macchia, *Baptized in the Spirit: A Global Pentecostal Theology* (Grand Rapids, MI: Zondervan, 2006), p. 218. The scope of the present essay does not allow for an in-depth analysis of the classical marks of the Church. Macchia's work offers an inspiring Pentecostal theological reflection on the marks of the Church (pp. 204-41) and the sacramental life of the faith community (pp. 241-56).

[10] Macchia, *Baptized in the Spirit*, p. 218.

[11] The Eastern Orthodox tradition has given us the vision of the Church as the icon of the Trinity on earth. Both personal human sociality and the Church's *koinonia* find their origin in the inner sociality of the Trinity and its mystical unity in diversity as the proto-community of love. Vladimir Lossky, *Orthodox Theology: An Introduction* (Crestwood, NY: St. Vladimir Seminary Press, 1978), p. 67. Ware, *The Orthodox Church*, pp. 240-42.

forecasts the eschatological unveiling of the cosmic lordship of the resurrected Christ before whom every knee shall bow, in heaven and on earth and under the earth; and whom every tongue shall confess (Phil. 2.10).

The Apostolicity of the Church is established by placing her birth in the context of the apostolic witness and teaching as articulated by Peter and the rest of the disciples at the event of Pentecost (Acts 2.14-40). Their first-hand witness of the risen Christ, through the voice and acts of His Body in the power of the Holy Spirit, spreads from Jerusalem throughout Judea and Samaria and to the uttermost parts of the world (Acts 1.8).

The radical Christocentricity of the event of Pentecost which shapes and marks the ecclesia as the Body of Christ, is consistent with the work of the Spirit as the agent who mediates, articulates, and leads all redemption history towards its eschatological fulfillment and summation in the risen Lord. Christ exemplifies 'the fullness of the deity' (Col. 2.9) as a communication of the Trinitarian life embodied within material existence. Therefore, the inclusion of the redeemed humanity into the Cosmic Christ is participation in the life of the communal Trinity within its Christic materiality as matter redeemed, renewed, and empowered by the Spirit. 'As the historical community of Christ, therefore, the Church is the eschatological creation of the Spirit'.[12] In the ecclesia, human history is met with its eschatological unfolding. Raptured and transfigured by the Spirit into the Kingdom of God, the Church becomes the sacred space where history is faced with its own future as the demand for and inevitability of transformation. The church is the embodiment of this future on earth and as such faces the world with the face of Christ as the ultimate destiny of all existence.[13]

---

[12] Jürgen Moltmann, *The Church in the Power of the Spirit* (Minneapolis, MN: Fortress Press, 1993), p. 33.

[13] Both Miroslav Volf (*After Our Likeness: The Church as the Image of the Trinity* [Grand Rapids, MI: Eerdmans, 1998], p. 128) and Frank Macchia (*Baptized in the Spirit*, pp. 209-11) affirm that the marks of the Spirit-baptized church are not drawn from the local or global dimensions of the ecclesia, but from the eschatological fulfillment of the gathering of the people of God in the new creation. Through the presence of the Spirit, this eschatological reality is experienced here and now. As Macchia asserts, this 'priority of the eschatological Spirit in determining the marks of the church explains why a local body can be filled with the Spirit with all grace' (p. 210).

The Pentecost event authenticates Christ's presence with and in His Body as the Baptizer with the Holy Spirit (Mk 1.8). The coming of the Spirit witnesses the completion of the redemptive work of Christ and transforms the community of faith into what it is truly called to be – a mission (Jn 15.26). For where Christ is, there is the Spirit through whom the Word becomes flesh and dwells among us – redeeming, healing, and renewing the world. And where the Spirit is, there is the *koinonia* of the Trinity extending its loving embrace in invitation to humanity to partake in the divine communal life and be transfigured into its likeness.

In view of the above, the present chapter offers a look at the event of Pentecost as the moment of birthing, anointing, and empowering the Body of Christ on earth to be a living extension of its resurrected Lord. In doing so, the chapter highlights the correlation between Pentecost, redemption, and sanctification and further reflects upon the significance of Pentecost in relation to the establishing of the Church as the icon of the Trinity on earth and as the visible image of the invisible Spirit. The chapter further examines the significance and liturgical function of speaking in tongues and the translatability of languages. It offers an understanding of *xenolalia* and *glossolalia* as an eschatological audible sign of the call to community with one another, and of heaven and earth in the Triune God, pointing to our ultimate eschatological destiny in Christ as the *omega* of all existence. Finally, the chapter advances a view of speaking in tongues as a form of liturgical *askesis* – of fasting from oneself on behalf of the other and the different from us. The practice of this spiritual discipline unites us with our eschatological *telos* in a prophetic proclamation of oneness with Christ as our personal and communal destiny. It asserts the advent of God's future in the midst of the Body of Christ as being the entrance to the new *aion* of the fullness of God's Kingdom on earth and marking the prophesying community of faith as the embodiment of the very future of the world.

The present theological reflection is rooted in the context of Eastern European Pentecostalism which, by virtue of its geographical location and spiritual heritage, has developed its theological content in continual dialogue with the Eastern Orthodox tradition. Therefore, the Eastern European Pentecostal view of the event of Pentecost and its ecclesiological significance does not emphasize

Pneumatology over or against Christology and holds a continual focus on the work of the Trinity, with all three persons simultaneously present in all events of the salvific history.

The text is further inspired by the liturgical life of the underground Pentecostal movement under communism. The community's informal sacramental theology recognized the suffering of the persecuted Church as the suffering of Christ and received it as a mark of discerning His Body on earth amidst an atheistic empire, viewed as representation of the spirit of antichrist. The believers' partaking of the divine nature translated into living each day as a sacrament of time, standing between the cross and the empty tomb – crucified and resurrected with Christ. In her self-under-standing as an extension of the suffering Christ on earth, the Church embodied her faith-witness with the pathos and *poesis* of Apostolic Christianity. The deep sense of the Church's mystical union with her Lord was articulated in her sacramental anamnesis. Through the agency of the Holy Spirit the sacraments united her with the life of Christ and made her a living sacrament in the world. She stood in the midst of the present as a prophetic negation and embodied proclamation of its inevitable social transformation, for she was an extension not only of the Suffering Servant, but also of the soon-coming King. In her He was arriving in the world.

Pentecost, Redemption, and Sanctification

In continuity with the Incarnation of the eternal Logos in the person of Christ, the event of Pentecost represents an explicit anti-gnostic statement – the Spirit embracing the materiality of 'all flesh' (Acts 2.17) within the life of the Triune God. As Vladimir Lossky points out, the

> profound meaning of the Incarnation resides in the physical and metaphysical vision of nature metamorphosed by grace, in this restoration henceforth acquired by human nature, in this breach opened through the opaqueness of death that leads to deification.[14]

[14] Lossky, *Orthodox Theology: An Introduction*, p. 92.

The Eastern Orthodox understanding of deification (*theosis*) as attaining the likeness of God in Christ-likeness is affirmed as the ultimate calling and purpose of all humanity.[15] The path towards the likeness of God demands one's continual Christic transfiguring which calls for sanctification of personal will and desires, for fasting from oneself on behalf of the other in expression of an incarnated love towards God and neighbor. The freedom of human will in the image of God is a prerequisite for attaining the divine likeness. As Lossky asserts, it takes one will to create humanity, but two to sanctify it. 'A single will to rise up the image, but two to make the image into a likeness'.[16] Therefore, sanctification demands the synergistic collaboration between the divine and human will. This synergy is impossible apart from Christ's incarnation, crucifixion, resurrection, and ascension. He is the Way (Jn 14.6) that bridges the chasm between humanity and God – the chasm of 'death, sin and fallen [human] nature.'[17] His incarnation overcomes the abyss of fallen nature; His crucifixion overcomes the chasm of sin; and as death is exhausted by His resurrection, the One who is the Resurrection and the Life (Jn 11.24) overcomes and destroys 'the last enemy' (1 Cor. 15.26).[18] Finally, in His ascension Christ unites heaven and earth as their ultimate destiny in and with God, bringing humanity within the *koinonia* of the Trinity, making us 'partakers of the divine nature' (2 Pet. 1.4) and making possible our transfiguring into its likeness. This vision of human destiny extends beyond the necessity of salvation into the eschatological goal of union with God in the Cosmic Christ (Eph. 1.10). United with Christ we participate in the immanence of His second coming, experiencing the transfiguration of the cosmos in 'the eternal splendor of the kingdom'.[19]

Therefore, sanctification as attaining the likeness of God manifests itself only as a result of the work of Christ (1 Cor. 1.30) – as an outcome of divine grace in and through the agency of the Holy Spirit (1 Pet. 1.2). 'The Holy Spirit is the main and essential begin-

---

15 Christophoros Stavropoulos, 'Partakers of Divine Nature', in Daniel B. Clendenin (ed.), *Eastern Orthodox Theology: A Contemporary Reader* (Grand Rapids, MI: Baker Books, 1995), pp. 183-84.

16 Lossky, *Orthodox Theology: An Introduction*, p. 73.

17 Stavropoulos, 'Partakers of Divine Nature', p. 188.

18 Stavropoulos, 'Partakers of Divine Nature', p. 188.

19 Lossky, *Orthodox Theology: An Introduction*, p. 85.

ning of sanctification'[20] – the One who applies what is objectively accomplished in Christ to the life of the individual believer and the community of faith, forming Christ's Body on earth.

Pentecost inaugurates the beginning of the sanctifying work of the Holy Spirit in the *koinonia* of redeemed humanity.[21] Therefore, Pentecost is not merely a continuation of the Incarnation or its sequel. It is its result and purpose. 'The creature has become fit to receive the Holy Spirit'[22] and be the dwelling place and in-fleshed reality of the Trinitarian *koinonia* in the cosmos. Therefore, as St. Basil asserts, the empowerment of the Holy Spirit is for 'perfection in holiness' as 'an unyielding, unchangeable commitment to goodness' – holiness as God-likeness that 'is impossible without the Spirit'.[23]

The Event of Pentecost as the Birthing, Anointing, and Empowering of the Body of Christ on Earth

The event of Pentecost could be viewed as the incarnation of Christ in the community of faith, a moment brought about through the agency of the Holy Spirit.[24] As the third person of the Trinity pours Himself over the one hundred twenty in the upper room, they become both Christ-bearers and a living extension of His resurrected Body on earth. Sergius Bulgakov has given us the image of Jesus' conception as being 'the Pentecost of the Virgin'.[25] As the Holy Spirit descends upon Mary in response to her willingness and readiness for service (Lk. 1.38), she is transformed into an instrument of God's Word becoming flesh amidst humanity (Jn 1.14). For Bulga-

---

[20] Stavropoulos, 'Partakers of Divine Nature', p. 188.

[21] Lossky, *Orthodox Theology: An Introduction*, p. 85.

[22] Lossky, *The Mystical Theology of the Eastern Church*, p. 159.

[23] St. Basil the Great, *On the Holy Spirit* (Crestwood, NY: St. Vladimir's Seminary Press, 1980), p. 63.

[24] Some of the content and insights of this particular section in the present chapter originated with my work on 'Pentecost as the Church's Cosmopolitan Vision of Civil Society', in William Storrar, Peter Casarella, and Paul Metzger (eds.), *A World for All? Global Civil Society in Political Theory and Trinitarian Theology* (Grand Rapids, MI: Eerdmans, 2011), pp. 197-220.

[25] Sergius Bulgakov, 'The Virgin and the Saints in Orthodoxy', pp. 65-75 in Daniel B. Clendenin (ed.), *Eastern Orthodox Theology: A Contemporary Reader* (Grand Rapids, MI: Baker Books, 1995), p. 67.

kov, it takes a willing human instrument to authenticate the humanness of Christ in the incarnation.[26]

In a similar manner, as the Spirit descends upon the disciples, Christ is conceived in them and they are empowered (Acts 1.8). Individually and corporately, they become Christ-bearers and bear forth an embodied gospel as a hope realized in the midst of a destitute humanity. The proclamation of the Good News is an announcement of God's providential presence with the hearers of the Word. It is an invitation to partake in the life of God and ultimately in the future of the world. The witness of the disciples on the day of Pentecost, 'speaking of the mighty deeds of God' (Acts 2.11), reminds us of Mary's Magnificat (Lk. 1.46-55). In both cases, it is the voice of the socially marginalized, ostracized, and persecuted. They announce the just socio-political reality of God's Kingdom, adventing among humanity in Jesus Christ, in whom the fulfillment of the divine covenantal promises of salvation (Lk. 1.54-55; Acts 2.33, 38-40) has been extended to all, even 'to the ends of the earth' (Acts 1.8).[27]

The Christocentrism of this event is further avowed through the transference of the messianic anointing from Christ to the community of faith. The community is His Body present in the world; they are thereby called and empowered to continue His mission and ministry outlined in the programmatic citation of Isaiah in Lk. 4.18-19.[28] In a manner similar to that in the narrative of Jesus' inauguration (Lk. 3.21-22), the Spirit of Pentecost descends upon His own – the incarnated Christ in His communal form – empowering the Body for the fulfillment of the messianic task. Therefore, the prophetic, royal, and priestly dimensions of Christ's ministry become an inseparable part of the charismatic reality of His Body, and the

---

[26] Bulgakov, 'The Virgin and the Saints in Orthodoxy', p. 67.

[27] Beverly Roberts Gaventa, *The Acts of the Apostles* (Abingdon New Testament Commentaries; Nashville, TN: Abingdon Press, 2003), p. 80.

[28] Roger Stronstad, *The Charismatic Theology of St. Luke* (Peabody, MA: Hendrickson, 1989), p. 59, draws the parallel between Pentecost and the transfer of the Spirit from Moses to the seventy elders (Num. 11.10-30). As Stronstad notes: 'Both narratives record the transfer of a leadership from a single individual to a group ... In both cases the transfer of the Spirit results in an outburst of prophesy.'

community of disciples is transformed into a royal priesthood and a prophethood of all believers.[29]

This incarnationalist view of Pentecost also allows us to consider the possibility of looking at the remainder of Acts as rooted in Christ's extended presence on earth in His Body. Therefore, if the Gospel of Luke represents the first volume of 'all that Jesus began to do and teach' (Acts 1.1), the book of Acts can be seen as the second volume outlining 'the continuation and fulfillment of what Jesus did and thought'.[30] Being a living extension of the risen Lord and continuation of His ministry in this world, the Body follows the extroverted orientation of Christ's mission, namely, from oneself towards the other. Therefore, for the community of faith, Pentecost is also a literal crossing of the bridge from the private to the public. As the Church moves beyond the enclosure of the Upper Room into the public space of the city and begins to participate in the civic discourse about the welfare of its citizens, it becomes a distinct factor of social change. This movement is also a crossing from the zone of mediation on the incarnated Christ to an incarnation of His presence. It is a transition from reflection (prayer) to interaction (witness) to action (transformation). It is a movement from 'the innermost being' (Jn 7.38) to the 'ends of the world' (Acts 1.8). Incarnation is the mode of this extroverted movement, and the Spirit is its agent, engine, and navigator. The Spirit's mission (in continuity with the character and nature of God) is realized through self-sharing – God pours Himself upon all flesh. In sharing His life, He becomes the source of life that sustains the spiritual ecology of the faith community.

---

[29] On the prophethood of the Pentecost Community see Roger Stronstad, *The Prophethood of All Believers* (JPTSup 16; Sheffield: Sheffield Academic Press, 1999), pp. 65-70.

[30] Matthias Wenk, *Community-Forming Power: The Socio-Ethical Role of the Spirit in Luke–Acts* (JPTSup 19; Sheffield: Sheffield Academic Press, 2000), p. 242. The author points to the outpouring of the Spirit at Pentecost as a clear example that the ministry of Christ (the Baptizer with the Holy Spirit) continues in Acts (p. 243) He mentions also the passages of Acts 9.5, 10; 13.39; 7.55-56; 17.7; 18.10; 19.15; and 25.19 as indicative of Jesus' acting upon the disciples. Another example is the healing of the beggar in Acts 3.1-16 'presented as a continuation of Jesus' healing ministry (Acts 4.30)' (p. 245). Beverly Gaventa's work also supports the view of the book of Acts as presenting a continuation of the ministry of Jesus. See her commentary *The Acts of the Apostles*, pp. 34, 62-63.

The event of Pentecost also ushers the revealing of the sons (and daughters) of God for which creation longs and groans (Rom. 8.20-23) in anticipation of justice, healing, and restoration. The Holy Spirit descended upon Jesus in His water baptism as a public statement of His identity as the Son of God – a statement of the love and approval of the Father for His only begotten Son (Mt. 3.17). The descent of the Spirit upon the Messiah was the identifier given to John the Baptist who proclaimed publicly Jesus' divine identity and mission (Jn 1.32-33).

In the same manner, the descending of the Holy Spirit upon the one hundred twenty on the Day of Pentecost is a public statement from the Father to His children of love and affirmation. They are indeed the sons and daughters of God and are, therefore, the recipients of the promise of the Father (Acts 2.39). This is the long anticipated eschatological unveiling of the identity of those who in their corporate existence as the Body of Christ on earth become the instruments of God's justice, healing, and restoration not only to human society but also to all the rest of creation. Through them the consequences of the life of God, in-fleshed in the community of faith, are translated to the rest of the created cosmos. The first Adam was responsible for the curse that permeated creation and its consequent pollution and distortion that has progressively intensified with humanity's multigenerational distance from Eden. The last Adam set free from the curse not only humanity, but also the rest of the created reality. The embodiment of this liberating truth in the Body of Christ on earth mandates it to carry forth the distributive justice of God towards creation. Thus, the ministry of reconciliation and its effects encompass not only the human *socium*, but also the rest of the created order – all material existence is brought in the redemptive embrace of the Trinity. Therefore, as Frank Macchia points out, Spirit baptism 'recalls God's Trinitarian openness to the world and the drama of how God would eventually pour the divine presence out in order to indwell all things through the role of the Son as the Spirit Baptizer'.[31] Pentecost marks the revealing of the children of God, and their presence on earth is manifested through God's therapeutic justice exercised through them toward all crea-

[31] Macchia, *Baptized in the Spirit*, p. 125.

tion summoned by the eschatological vision of the Cosmic Christ. Therefore, on the Day of Pentecost Spirit Baptism exhibits the teleological tension of the 'already' and 'not yet' of the Kingdom reality and points to its apocalyptic 'culmination with the Day of the Lord'.[32] As God subjects all things to Christ (1 Cor. 15.28), He delivers creation from death unto eternal life, by indwelling it with His own life in the Spirit and 'making all things new' (Rev. 21.5).

Pentecost and the Establishing of the Church as the Icon of the Trinity

On the day of Pentecost,

> A new reality came into the world – the Church, founded on a two-fold divine economy: the work of Christ and the work of the Holy Spirit ... The work of both is requisite that we may attain to union with God.[33]

The Son makes the union of humanity with God once again possible through His incarnation, death, resurrection, and ascension; overcoming sin, death, and the grave. The Spirit bestows the fullness of this union upon each one of the believers, binding them together into one Body whose head is Christ (Eph. 4.15). The Son recapitulates humanity into Himself[34] – into His Body, the Church – as the new corporal existence of the redeemed. The corporal unity of the faith community is the prerequisite of the Spirit's *kenosis*, yet the tongues of fire distribute themselves and rest upon each one of the believers (Acts 2.1-3). The singularity of the Church proceeds from the singularity of Christ. The event is Christoforming and, therefore, Christocentric. Yet the Spirit celebrates, sustains, and gardens the diversity of different persons within the charismatic singularity of the Son's Body, making possible its simultaneous oneness and catholicity. While Christ brings about the unity, the

---

[32] Macchia, *Baptized in the Spirit*, p. 102.

[33] Lossky, *The Mystical Theology of the Eastern Church*, p. 156.

[34] St. Irenaeus, *Against Heresies*, book IV, ch. XIV, in *The Apostolic Fathers with Justin Martyr and Irenaeus*, Christian Classics Ethereal Library (http://www.ccel.org/ccel/schaff/anf01.ix.vii.xv.html).

Spirit mediates and sustains the diversity. The singular is preserved within the communal.

As the Spirit distributes Himself upon each separate believer, He translates the mystery of the Trinitarian life into the community of faith – the mystery of the One God in the plurality of three hypostases – the mystery of diversity in unity. Thus, the Church becomes an icon of the unique divine life embodied within the human *socium*. She becomes the image of God on earth.

Yet, since the fullness of the deity resides in each separate person of the Trinity, on the day of Pentecost, the *kenosis* of the Spirit saturates each member of the Body with the fullness of the divine presence, sealing their unique relationship with the Triune God. Thus the Trinitarian life becomes present in the community of faith both corporately and personally. The indwelling of the separate believer by the Spirit, transforms his/her being into 'the throne of the Holy Trinity, for the Father and the Son are inseparable from the deity of the Spirit'.[35] Thus, the Spirit conceives the Kingdom of God within humanity, for the Kingdom is the sovereign reign of God in us.

Therefore, the Pentecost descent of the Holy Spirit inaugurates the transfiguring of this world into the Kingdom of God. As the Kingdom takes its residence in humanity, it grows within until it overtakes one's entire life, transforming it into Christ-likeness so that no longer we, but Christ, lives in us (Gal. 2.20); until the life of God has become our life on earth (Rev. 11.15). The Kingdom overflows from us into the world until it covers it as the waters of the sea (Heb. 2.14) until all flesh is saturated by the kenosis of the Spirit and Christ – the fullness of God in flesh – becomes all in all (Eph. 1.10).

If the Church is an image of the Trinity, she is also the image of the Holy Spirit. The Spirit descends upon the community of faith, bearing witness to the Son (Jn 15.26). He comes in the name of the Son in the way the Son comes in the name of the Father. As Lossky states,

> The divine Persons do not themselves assert themselves, but one bears witness to another. It is for this reason that St. John

[35] Lossky, *The Mystical Theology of the Eastern Church*, p. 171.

Damascene said that 'the Son is the image of the Father, and the Spirit the image of the Son.'[36]

The Holy Spirit, however, does not have His image made visible in another person (or hypostasis). Yet, the event of Pentecost made the invisible Spirit visible in the Spirit-saturated community of faith; for indeed, it takes a community to make visible the image of the Spirit as the communal life of the Trinity within the charismatic Body of the resurrected Messiah. If the Old Testament 'proclaimed the Father openly, but the Son more obscurely' and the Gospels reveal the Son plainly, but the Spirit dimly,[37] Pentecost presents the Church animated and empowered by the Spirit as His clearly manifested image on earth. The charismatic dynamic of the Church makes the invisible Spirit visible and tangibly communicated in the unity of the saints' diversity.

Therefore, the two distinct dimensions of the Spirit's presence, the communal and the eschatological,[38] become clearly visible in the Pentecost inauguration of the Church as His image on earth. Pentecost ushers the unfolding of the *eschata* evoking the prophetic fusion of time and eternity as the 'last days' erupt into the present and become its time-transcending substance. Yet, this eschatological vision is the vision of the Spirit-saturated community with its radical egalitarian catholicity and democratized polyphony of prophetic utterance – the communal voice of God in the concert articulation of His Word (Acts 2.17-18). The creative power of the Word brings about the reality of the Kingdom in the present through the voices of the Spirit-filled community. Only the Spirit can sustain the significance of the individual voice in the communal symphony, empowering each voice across all demographic boundaries.

The Pentecost Church stands in the present as the very future of the world, exemplifying the mystery of the Trinitarian communal life in the community of the saints as the ultimate calling and destiny of all creation. The Spirit's orientation is always towards the *es-*

---

36 Lossky, *The Mystical Theology of the Eastern Church*, p. 160.

37 St. Gregory of Nazianzus, *The Fifth Theological Oration. On the Holy Spirit*, XXVI, in *Cyril of Jerusalem and Gregory of Nazianzen*, *Christian Classics Ethereal Library* (http:// www.ccel.org/ccel/schaff/npnf207.iii.xvii.html).

38 John D. Zizioulas, *Being as Communion: Studies in Personhood and the Church* (Crestwood, NY: St. Vladimir's Seminary Press, 1995), p. 131.

chaton as He mediates the embodiment of the future into the present until the present is outgrown and overtaken by it. Yet Christ, the *omega* of all existence, is the final summation of the future – the fullness of the last things as the ultimate purpose of all salvation history. The Spirit moves history forth towards this *telos*, evoking the 'Christification' of the cosmos, until Christ is all in all (Eph. 1.23). The Church is the incarnational vehicle of this divinely ordained transfiguring of the world. The Spirit draws the Body together one person at the time, reaching into the world through the Body of Christ and welcoming it into the embrace of the Triune God – into the fellowship of the Trinitarian proto-community. Thus, the Body of the crucified and resurrected Christ in the power of the Holy Spirit becomes a living gospel to the world proclaiming the life of God as the life of the redeemed human community and leading the world into its divine reality.

Speaking in Tongues and the Translatability of Human Language

Babel and the Eruption of the Language of the Other

Christian Theology has a long-standing tradition of viewing the event of Pentecost as an overcoming or a reversal of Babel.[39] The connection between the two events, however, can be also seen in the continuity of God's prophetic deconstruction of every imperial consciousness that is inherently homogenizing and violently marginalizing of those who are other and different.[40]

The account in Genesis 11 describes the architectonic of an empire suppressing all differences that attempt to destabilize its own grand project for self-immortalization. The text contrasts the speech and action of the empire (vv. 2-4) with the speech-act of God (vv. 5-8). The imperial project looks for shortcuts to its goal of totalizing uniformity. Substituting 'brick for stone and tar for mortar' (v. 3), the architects of empire hurry to mark a territory and establish dominion. In order to assume superiority over the 'plain of

---

[39] On the view of Pentecost as a reversal of Babel see Avery Dulles, *The Catholicity of the Church* (Oxford: Oxford University Press, 1987), p. 173.

[40] Miroslav Volf, *Exclusion and Embrace: A Theological Exploration of Identity, Otherness and Reconciliation* (Nashville, TN: Abingdon Press, 1996), pp. 226-31.

Shinar', they use imperial propaganda that cultivates in the populace a fear of the future and of the other. The boundaries of empire are presented as the demarcations of safety (v. 4). Beyond them is 'the face of the whole world' (v. 4), which is a special designation for the location of *the face of the other*.[41] 'Heaven' (v. 4) is the ultimate goal of the project; the empire has identified itself with the final, undisputed authority. With that move nothing remains beyond its scope. Sacred space collapses in its grip and leaves humanity with no exodus from the totalitarian order.

As God comes down in the plurality of personhood expressed by the divine speech ('let us', v. 7), He acts in conformity with His nature of creating and affirming diversity. He extends self-giving by opening space and time for the other and thereby creates the possibility of an authentic human community, one in which life can be shared together in a multiplicity of forms and locations. In view of that, the destruction of the empire's project is an act of deconstructing a world order that has eliminated the possibility of the other. God induces this imperial collapse by bringing the language of the other forth within the homogeneity of human space. The monotone superiority of imperial culture is challenged by the polyphony of human speech as the inaugural address of a multicultural human reality (vv. 7, 9). The demanding immediacy of the other's presence brings about the demolition of the empire's boundaries, as the formerly homogenized population overflows and spreads 'abroad over the face of the whole earth' (v. 9). The possibility of human community after Babel becomes a function of learning the language of the other. The actualization of the human *telos* depends on the commitment to make space for the existence of the different. After all, according to God's providential plan, there is no salvation without the other.

The confusion following the eruption of the other (v. 9) will accompany humanity in its journey after Babel. Fallen human nature continues to gravitate to the homogenizing shortcuts of empire,

---

[41] The immediate association of this phrase is with the work of Emmanuel Levinas and his emphasis on the other as the focal point of ethics, and of ethics as being the first philosophy. The face of the other, as an expression of their presence, summons us to responsibility and justice becomes defined as our relationship to the other.

offering its dehumanizing patterns of association as a substitute for the need of sociality in the diversity of authentic human community. God's alternative, designed to bring the restoration of His communion with humanity (and of authentic human sociality as a reflection of the restoration of His image in human beings) situates salvation within the relationship to the other (Exod. 20.12-17). From the midst of 'the thunder and lightening flashes and the sound of the trumpet and the mountain smoking' at Sinai (Exod. 20.18), God establishes in a creative speech-act a covenant with His people. The divine utterance unites the aural and visual dimensions of human communication, and His flaming words become visible to the multitude (similar to the burning bush experience of Moses in Exod. 3.2-5, and later to the flames of Pentecost in Acts 2.3).[42] He brings the other into the center of personal and corporate social redemption (Deut. 5.16-21; Exod. 20.12-17). The appropriation of the covenant bond with God demands the establishment of covenantal bonds with the other – the immediate other (one's mother, father, neighbor) as well as the distant other (the stranger, the foreigner, the gentile). God remains in our midst as the omnipresent Other in whom we move and live and have our being (Acts 17.28). Therefore, we see in the Sinai event the establishment of a communal covenant as an immediate embodiment and extension of the salvific covenant with God.

God's words have the unique quality of embodying a creative force that bespeaks reality. As such, they stand before the people not only as a covenantal demand (or a command) but also as a promise. The hearers of the words can love God and neighbor as the Holy Spirit engraves the law on their hearts, and they are there-

---

[42] In his commentary on Acts, Luke Timothy Johnson points to the symbolism utilized by Philo Judaeus, 'who explicitly attaches the giving of the Law by God to the communication of speech by flame'. Johnson offers the following quotation of his work (*On the Decalogue*): 'Then from the midst of the fire that streamed from heaven there sounded forth to their utter amazement a voice, for the flame became articulated speech in the language familiar to the audience, and so clearly and distinctly were the words formed by it that they seemed to see rather than hear them'. *The Acts of the Apostles* (Collegeville, MN: A Michael Glazier Book, The Liturgical Press, 1992), p. 46.

by transformed into His likeness.[43] The fulfillment of the promise is already initiated in the moment of its impartation, for God and His Word already inhabit the future. In the immutability of the divine presence, the proclamation of the promise becomes an articulated preview of its fulfillment.

The event of Pentecost could be understood in relation to the promised fulfillment of a renewed covenant with God and neighbor (Jer. 31.33) that is brought about through God's transformational self-giving.[44] The covenant has been established in God's self-giving in Christ and sealed with His self-giving in the Spirit that brings the believers into the *koinonia* of the Trinity and makes them partakers of the divine nature.

Therefore, as outlined in Peter's sermon (Acts 2.14-39), the incarnation, crucifixion, resurrection, and ascension of Christ are central to the Pentecost theophany of the Spirit. Pentecost authenticates the redemption accomplished by God on behalf of humanity in Christ Jesus. Christ is the new Adam (1 Cor. 15.45), the perfect icon and representation of God (Col. 1.15, 2 Cor. 4.4). In Him humanity is thus restored to its proper position in relation to the divine and the rest of creation. Human sociality is redeemed in com-

---

[43] Leonid Ouspensky, 'The Meaning of and Content of the Icon,' pp. 33-63 in D.B. Clendenin (ed.), *Eastern Orthodox Theology* (Grand Rapids, MI: Baker Books, 1995), pp. 37-38.

[44] Reflecting on the connection between the giving of the Torah and the celebration of Pentecost, Luke T. Johnson states that: 'After the destruction of the temple in CE 70, it is clear that Pentecost was universally understood by the Jews to be the celebration of the giving of the Torah on Mt. Sinai' (*The Acts of the Apostles*, p. 46). Roger Stronstad points out that the feast of Pentecost was historically celebrated as 'the second of three pilgrim festivals in Israel's liturgical calendar' (*The Prophethood of All Believers: A Study in Luke's Charismatic Theology*, p. 54). Regarding the possibility that Luke's account on Pentecost was influenced by the rabbinic tradition equating the feast of Pentecost with the giving of the Law, Stronstad suggests that it is unlikely, since this rabbinic tradition developed later than the Pentecost narrative in Acts (*The Charismatic Theology of St. Luke*, p. 58). The rabbinic tradition eventually developed the belief that when the law was given, it was heard not only by Israel but also by the 72 nations listed in Gen. 10.2-31. In his commentary on Acts, F.F. Bruce cites the Midrash Tanchuma 26C, that at Sinai the voice of God divided into 'seven voices and then went into seventy tongues' (*Commentary on the Book of Acts* [NICNT; Grand Rapids, MI: Eerdmans, 1979], p. 60). In opposition to Stronstad, Johnson points out that 'Luke certainly could have made the connection' between the Pentecost feast and the giving of the Torah, on his own, in spite of the existence or not of such a tradition prior to his account of Pentecost in Acts.

munion with the other as a reflection and extension through the Holy Spirit of the trinitarian life of God.[45] Therefore, the charismatic *koinonia* of the believers represents a renewal of the communal covenant within the context of the restoration in Christ of the salvific covenant between humanity and the Redeeming Trinity.

As Pentecost marks the moment of the historical realization of the promise of covenantal renewal with God and neighbor, language and its translatability becomes once again the symbolic center of the event as an audible manifestation of God's *telos* for humanity and the rest of creation.

The Translatability of Language as a Call to Community

It is no accident that the language of the other stands at the center of the Pentecost event as an expression of the prioritization of the other in the Kingdom of a new humanity. In the words of Mikhail Bakhtin, '... language, for the individual consciousness, lies on the borderline between oneself and the other'.[46] Language participates in the composition of one's personal and corporate identity and therefore could be viewed as being 'constitutive to reality and not just a reflection of it'.[47] Jean-François Lyotard reminds us that the translatability of language points to the fact that all human beings are called to one speech community.[48] The translation of language is not a mere tool for transforming an obscure sound into a coherent thought. It is a path to convergence of contents and identities into a dialogical whole which takes a life of its own. In this new mutual conversational identity there is a purpose and a destiny shared by the participants. The participation in the language of the other becomes a participation in their identity and future as our own.

---

45 For an in-depth discussion on the Trinitarian sociality as expressed in the human socium, see: Miroslav Volf, *After Our Likeness: The Church in the Image of the Trinity* (Grand Rapids, MI: Eerdmans, 1998). Also see Владимир Соловьёв, 'Троичное Начало и его Общественно Приложение', pp. 243-334, in *Чтения о Богочеловечество* (Санкт-Петербург: Азбука, 2000), esp. in Chapter 10, Soloviov's passage on the Social Trinity.

46 Mikhail Bakhtin, 'Discourse in the Novel', in Michael Holquist (ed.), *The Dialogic Imagination* (Austin, TX: The University of Texas Press, 1981), p. 293.

47 Maria Teresa Morgan, 'Tongues as of Fire: The Spirit as Paradigm for Ministry in a Multicultural Setting', in Bradford E. Hinze (ed.), *The Spirit in the Church and the World* (New York: Orbis Books, 2004), p. 107.

48 J.-F. Lyotard, 'The Other's Rights,' in S. Shute and S. Hurley (ed.), *On Human Rights* (New York: Basic Books, 1993), pp. 140-41.

Bakhtin's idea of *heteroglossia* is a useful concept in exploring the corporate and personal social effects of dialogization. Bakhtin points out that words are not neutral and impersonal.[49] Language is historically and ideologically specific.[50] Yet, his view of the dialogization of languages reaches further than the Socratic debate or the Hegelian dialectic. Dialogical *heteroglossia* creates a multidimensional unity of oneself with the other while preserving the distinctiveness of each one. On the one hand, the word we speak is always 'half someone else's'.[51] On the other hand, the words we speak become populated with the intentions of the other (as well as with our own), for language is always directed towards understanding of the other.[52]

If the translatability of languages are a call to community, then we can examine, in light of this assertion, the communal summoning within the *xenolalic* and *glossolalic* dimensions of speech convergence.

Xenolalia and *Glossolalia* as the First Audible Sign of Our Eschatological Destiny

The *xenolalic* translatability of languages at the event of Pentecost points to the eschatological destiny of humanity as being called to one human community in the household of God. All of us are His offspring (Acts 17.28) sharing a common origin and purpose. 'God in the Spirit is God existing in community',[53] and the event of Pentecost as the authentic work of the Spirit is expressed in His building the bonds of the charismatic *koinonia* and renewing the communal covenant within the spiritual context of God's salvific covenant. The Spirit empowers humanity to recover the speech of the other across lines of alienation and mutual exclusion into a 'covenantal conversation that fosters the root form of human relatedness: communion'.[54] His therapeutic presence deconstructs stereotypes and walls of divisions across gender, class, ethnicity, and language

---

49 Bakhtin, *The Dialogic Imagination*, p. 294.

50 Bakhtin, *The Dialogic Imagination*, p. 294.

51 Bakhtin, *The Dialogic Imagination*, p. 293.

52 Bakhtin, *The Dialogic Imagination*, p. 282.

53 Peter Hodgson, *Winds of the Spirit: A Constructive Christian Theology* (Louisville, KY: Westminster/John Knox Press, 1994), p. 296.

54 Eleasar S. Fernandez, 'From Babel to Pentecost: Finding a Home in the Belly of Empire', *Semeia* 90/91 (Spring-Summer 2002), p. 41.

divides and ministers healing and wholeness to individuals and communities. Therefore, Pentecost could be viewed as a redemptive eschatological recovery of Eden[55] where the community of the Trinity is once again the community of humanity and the rest of creation; where humanity is restored into harmony with one another and God in a radical communal unity of diversity as the Spirit makes all things new.

In view of this conclusion, we can discuss the significance of the *glossolalic* translatability as the converging of the tongues of heaven and earth. Illuminated by the vision of the final eschatological unity of all existence in Christ, the charismatic practice of *glossolalia* (and interpretation) may be viewed as a foretaste of the ultimate destiny of heaven and earth as being called together into one holy *koinonia.* It points to the teleological joining of the terrestrial and celestial in Christ and, therefore, in His church as the new redeemed community of the Spirit. The charismatic gift unites the material and spiritual dimensions of existence – the visible and the invisible reality. It manifests the Church as the new creation in which heaven and earth are reunited in the life of the Triune God. Therefore, the Spirit-baptized church becomes the embodied experience of heaven on earth – heaven transforming and transfiguring the earth into the Kingdom of God.

The Kingdom, as the sovereign rule of God, summons the hosts of heaven and earth in the unity of the Spirit within the liturgy of the Church. Thus, in her worship and work (*leitourgia*) the Church becomes the future of the world, as well as the spiritual location where the once invisible celestial realm is made present, transparent, and visible. *Glossolalia* is an audible sign of this eschatological unfolding within the Body of Christ – the mutual indwelling of heaven and earth as the foretaste of their ultimate Christic destiny.

The liturgy of the Church celebrates this union as its very essence and self-expression. The liturgical worship of the community of faith is not only a portal to heaven but also a merging of the celestial and earthly celebration of God's presence. There is one altar, one sacrifice, one presence, and all the invisible host of heaven joins the redeemed humanity around that altar – the table of the

---

[55] Vigen Guroian, 'Fruits of Pentecost: The Christian Gardener', *The Christian Century* 113.21 (July 3, 1996), pp. 684-86.

Lord. We worship surrounded by 'the great cloud of witnesses' (Heb. 12.1), our spiritual eyes open to the nearness of the angels and the saints from all generations standing with us around the throne of God Who meets us in the familiar face of Christ – the incarnated eternal Word, the Lamb of God, the *Pantokrator* of all (Rev. 1.8).

Therefore, both *xenolalia* and *glossolalia* have a sacramental function in the life of the charismatic community,[56] articulating the mystery of the union of the redeemed creation with its Creator and experiencing the in-breaking of the eschatological fullness of Christ in His Body. It is an experience of the presence and self-sharing of God in His Spirit that welcomes us in the life of the Trinity and makes us an extension of His life on earth.

Speaking in Tongues as Liturgical *Askesis*

In embracing the language of the other, the speaker surrenders to the movement of the Spirit who shapes the oneness of the Body in its Christ-likeness. The translatability of languages has already pointed to this sacramental oneness – the unity of heaven and earth and all humanity in Christ as the *omega* of all existence (Rev. 1.8).

The initial surrender of our tongue to the language of the other (both *xenolalic* and *glossolalic*) is an expression of embracing this call to oneness in Christ as our personal and communal destiny. Therefore, the continual practice of speaking in tongues by the believer could be viewed as an act of *praktikê* (ascetic struggle) within the context of liturgy. These are acts of fasting from oneself on behalf of the other in sacramental gestures of proclaiming the will of God as one's freely chosen destiny – the redemptive joining of all creation in the One Christ until He is 'all in all' (Eph. 1.23). This proc-

---

[56] Frank Macchia's work on speaking in tongues as a sacrament offers important insights into the liturgical practice of the charismatic gift. See his essay 'Tongues as a Sign: Towards a Sacramental Understanding of Tongues', *Pneuma* 15.1 (Spring 1993), pp. 61-76. As Kenneth Archer has stated, the sacraments 'are prophetic narrative signs involving words and deeds through which the community can experience the redemptive living presence of God in Christ through the Holy Spirit' ('Nourishment for Our Journey: The Pentecostal *Via Salutis* and Sacramental Ordinances', *JPT* 13.1 [2004], p. 86). Archer's definition clearly applies to both *xenolalia* and *glossolalia* as discussed in the present essay.

lamation is consistent with the understanding of theology 'as internal vision, which requires personal, ascetic effort'. It requires not only an individual, but also a communal effort, 'an effort made within the community of saints'.[57] This is the eschatological vision of the Cosmic Christ, which becomes a 'Christoforming'[58] force in the life of the faith community. This ascetic effort asserts that 'He must increase', but we 'must decrease' (Jn 3.30) so that the reality of the Kingdom may become the reality of our life in the Spirit-formed *koinonia* with God and neighbor.

As Margaret Pfeil asserts, *praktikê* takes place

> as the Christian worshiper's graced and free response to God's gratuitous love celebrated in Christian liturgy. First, liturgical asceticism springs from and seeks to nourish the life of the Christian worshiping community, and second, it implies an eschatological horizon in which the ultimate *telos* of *askesis* consists in the fullness of life in God.[59]

Speaking in tongues is, therefore, also a prophetic assertion of the inevitability of God's future and its *parousia* in the community of faith. It is an evidence of the coming of God as the Holy Spirit takes residence in the Body of Christ and articulates through its voice the presence of the Kingdom on earth.

The sacramental life of the Church in its liturgical expression has been described in terms of 'eschatological symbolism'.[60] As Alexander Schmemann points out, in the early Christian community the 'eschatological' meaning was defined as the belief that

> the coming of Christ, His life, His death and resurrection from the dead, His ascension to heaven and the sending by Him, on the day of Pentecost, of the Holy Spirit, have brought about the

---

[57] John Meyendorff, 'Doing Theology in an Eastern Orthodox Perspective', pp. 79-96, in Daniel B. Clendenin (ed.), *Eastern Orthodox Theology: A Contemporary Reader* (Grand Rapids, MI: Baker Books, 1995), p. 87.

[58] The term is used by Frank Macchia in *Baptized in the Spirit*, p. 106.

[59] Pfeil, 'Liturgy and Ethics', pp. 127-49, and there pp. 127-28.

[60] Alexander Schmemann, *Liturgy and Tradition* (ed. Thomas Fish; Crestwood, NY: St. Vladimir's Seminary Press, 1990), p. 125.

Lord's Day; the *Yom Yahweh* announced by the prophets has inaugurated the new *aeon* of the Kingdom of God.[61]

In its union with Christ, as His Body anointed with the Holy Spirit, the Church already indwells this new *aeon* and manifests it on earth as the embodied future. Therefore, the sacramental eschatological symbolism has as essential particularity 'the fact that in it the very distinction between the sign and the signified is simply ignored'. In it 'the sign and that which it signifies are one and the same thing'.[62] In a way, 'the liturgy happens to us', since the liturgical entrance is 'the church's entrance to heaven'.[63] Because we are *in* Christ, we are one with Him in the unfolding of the *eschata* within the present, which transforms the sacramental life of the Church into a realized eschatology. As the Church walks through the present as a prophetic unfolding of its eschatological destiny, the sacraments articulate the three continual movements in her liturgical life: her ascent to heaven to the table of the Lord and His sustaining loving presence, her descent to earth carrying in her midst the reality of heaven so that there may be heaven on earth that welcomes all humanity in the embrace of God, and finally her going out into the world to proclaim the gospel and share the reality of the Kingdom – of redemption, healing, and restoration, until it covers the earth as the waters of the sea (Hab. 2.14).

As Frank Macchia points out, through the agency of the Holy Spirit 'we participate in that which signifies the sanctification of creation to become the very dwelling place of God through the crucifixion and resurrection of the Spirit Baptizer'.[64] Therefore the sacramental practice of *xenolalia* and *glossolalia* mediates to us the power of the invisible grace that transforms us into a visible extension of Christ on earth, making us co-sharers in the life of God and through it in one another as the Body of Christ.

---

61 Schmemann. *Liturgy and Tradition*, p. 125.
62 Schmemann. *Liturgy and Tradition*, p. 127.
63 Schmemann. *Liturgy and Tradition*, p. 127.
64 Macchia, *Baptized in the Spirit*, p. 253.

Instead of Conclusion: Eden, Babel and Pentecost in the Story of Personal and Communal Salvation

A number of the Early Fathers of the Church differentiated between the 'image' and the 'likeness' of God in humanity as His creation.[65] The image is understood as a God-given potentiality of likeness, while the likeness, culminating in union with God, is seen as the final goal and destiny of human existence. The likeness is an outcome of cooperation and alignment of the free human will with the will of God. Thus, attaining the likeness is a process and an empowering pedagogy on becoming like God by choosing to love and will like Him. It is a call to perfection substantiated by uncreated grace that makes humanity partaker in the divine nature.

In light of that, the story of the Fall in the Garden of Eden could be viewed as a narrative of humanity's free choice to reject God's way towards attaining His likeness and take, instead, a pseudo 'short cut' towards fulfilling its destiny. Therefore, the desire of Adam and Eve to become like God (Gen 3.5) is a God-given ontological impetus reflecting their purpose as creatures. Yet, there is only one way for the creature to become like the Creator – the Creator's way of participation in His life, until the life of the deity becomes the life of His creation. There is not a 'short cut', or a magical fruit that can spring this likeness in one's being. It takes life in covenantal communion with God as a perpetual surrender of one's existence on earth to the divine *telos,* as an incarnational enactment of His will in the human being, until he/she becomes an extension of God's life on earth.

The 'likeness of God' is, therefore, the fullness of a communion and community with God. It is the fullness of participation in the divine nature as partaking in the proto-community of the Holy Trinity. Being created in the image of the divine community and for the purpose of participation in its communal life, humanity is called not only individually but corporately to develop the divine communal likeness. Therefore, the likeness of God demands communal redemption. Sanctification is always social.

---

[65] Lossky, *The Mystical Theology of the Eastern Church*, pp. 114-21.

In continuity with this reflection, the story of the tower of Babel can be seen as a narrative of the communal dimension of humanity's drama first enacted in the Garden of Eden. It is the story of human society searching, this time corporately, for a 'short cut' of ascent into heaven through the vehicle of its civilizational evolution. This is an ascent that aims to translate the life of heaven into the life of the human *socium* on earth. It is a pursuit of the likeness of God through human means. Yet, once again, there is no such thing as a 'short cut' that can bring the life of God in and among humanity.

At Babel humanity counterfeits its calling, the likeness of the Triune God, by sacrificing authentic community on the altar of imperial expediency. The true communal likeness of God necessitates diversity in unity, based on equality and freedom to be and to become out of one's free will an extension of the divine communal life on earth. In contrast, the imperial propaganda of Babel eliminates diversity, flattening it into a monotonous uniformity, into a compressed homogeneity induced by fear for survival in the presence of the other and the different (Gen. 11.4). Therefore, by deconstructing the project of imperial uniformity, God creates the conditions for initiating authentic human community through bringing forth the existence of the other and establishing the communal necessity of diversity in unity (Gen. 11.7-8). The new accomplishment of human community after Babel demands accepting the other and making the effort to learn his or her language. This is God's response to the totalizing uniformity of imperial consciousness – a response inseparable from His providential plan for the salvation of humanity.

Like the story of humanity's Fall in the Garden of Eden, the narrative of Babel reasserts the conviction that the advent of the Kingdom of God on earth as the life of God in and among humanity is God's own doing. It cannot be brought about by human effort and imperial infrastructural projects, but only by the Spirit of God. For only the Spirit conceives the divine likeness in humanity and translates heaven on earth until this world is transfigured into the Kingdom of God.

In light of the above, the event of Pentecost marks the Spirit's initiation of the likeness of God in humanity, both personally and corporately. The redemption of humanity in Christ is a necessary prerequisite for the restoration of the potentiality to fulfill its true *telos* of becoming like God in becoming like Christ. The last Adam reversed the consequences of the Fall by rejecting the temptation to take a short-cut towards attaining one's calling (Lk. 4.1-13). Thus, Christ incarnated the will of God as the only way to heaven on earth, the only way to the lost paradise of life in and with the communal God.

In the same way the self-pouring of the Holy Spirit on the Day of Pentecost reverses the consequences of Babel's imperial project, by reaffirming God's salvific work as redemption of the human community, empowering it to choose and embody the life of God on earth as diversity in unity sustained by love towards God and neighbor. As Lossky states:

> Pentecost is thus the object, the final goal of the divine economy upon earth. Christ returns to the Father that the Spirit may descend (Jn 16.7).[66]

Yet, from the beginning, 'it was God's intention to bring all things in heaven and on earth to a unity in Christ, and each of us participates in this great movement'.[67] This process is one of 'the "Christification" of the whole cosmos'.[68] Beyond the historical horizon stands the cosmic Christ, and the Church in the power of the Spirit is His living extension in the present, welcoming the world as the embodiment of its future – the future of humanity in the likeness of God.

---

[66] Lossky, *The Mystical Theology of the Eastern Church*, p. 159.

[67] Desmond Tutu, *No Future without Forgiveness* (New York: Doubleday, 2000), p. 265.

[68] Jürgen Moltmann, *Jesus Christ for Today's World* (Minneapolis, MN: Fortress Press, 1994), p. 101. Moltmann picks up the idea of cosmic evolving towards Christ from Teilhard de Chardin's 'Christ the Evolver' in *Christianity and Evolution* (trans. R. Hugue; London: Collins, 1971).

2

The Cosmopolitanism of Divine Welcome: The Hospitality of God, Justice, and the Other

The process of globalization, as the technologically induced compression of time and space, has brought us face to face with once upon a time distant dwellers in ways that just a few decades ago were only the subject of science-fiction. Globalization has shrunk the 'safe' distance between us and the total stranger. It has changed (seemingly overnight) the demographics of our neighborhoods, and has challenged us with the demanding immediacy of the language and face of the other. The world has arrived in our backyard along with the realization that we all share a global household and a responsibility for its health and functionality. There is an escalating sense of urgency that our survival as a human race depends on our ability to transform the multicultural polyphony of the globe into a purposeful dialogue motivated by a cosmopolitan vision of a just future. Our striking cultural diversity, situated among the pressing transnational realities of poverty, genocide, ethnic and religious hatred, and terrorism, shows that institutionalized multiculturalism is central to any viable global transformation. Yet, as humanity struggles to translate and expand the ideas of democracy from the dimensions of the nation-state to those of the global village, we continually encounter the discrepancies between ideals and their institutionalization and witness the inabilities of international institutions to achieve their inaugural visions.[1]

Amidst a rising sense of socio-political claustrophobia under the influx of the other, the West has occasionally manifested its social anxiety in the pathological form of xenophobia, feeling threatened and repelled by the stranger. Yet, Western civilization with its human rights tradition stands upon the foundation of a Judeo-Christian culture, whose sacred texts are marked by unapologetic preoccupation with justice for the other. Scripture mandates the practice of hospitality (in Greek, *philoxenia* – or literally 'love for strangers') as benevolence and justice for the other – the orphan, the widow, the impoverished, the foreigner, and the sojourner. The covenantal relation between God and His people demands one's continual economic and socio-political re-spacing for the sake of the other, not only when they are like us, but also when they are completely different from us. This covenant-instituted hospitality to foreigners does not demand their conversion and cultural conformity before experiencing the gift of hospitality. Strangers and foreigners are given access to life as an experience of God's justice healing the fractures of a world estranged and traumatized by violent conflicts.[2]

Letty M. Russel states that hospitality is 'solidarity with strangers'[3] and 'expression of unity without uniformity' through which 'community is built out of difference and not sameness'.[4] However, when understood in terms of *philoxenia*, hospitality seems to be unnatural, or at least counterintuitive. To love the strangers means to accept them unconditionally as who they are and not in light of anticipating their transformation into our own likeness. Our intuition provokes distance and suspicion toward the stranger. We

---

[1] Mayda Yegenoglou, 'Liberal Multiculturalism and the Ethics of Hospitality in the Age of Globalization', *Postmodern Culture* (http://www3.iath.virginia.edu/pmc/issue.103/13.2yegenoglu.html); David Lloyd in 'Race under Representation', *Oxford Literary Review* 13.1-2 (1991), p. 70; Slavoj Zizek, 'Multiculturalism', *New Left Review* 225 (September/October 1997), pp. 28-51.

[2] Letty M. Russel, *Just Hospitality: God's Welcome in a World of Difference* (Louisville, KY: John Knox Press, 2009), p. 19. Russel defines hospitality as 'the practice of God's welcome by reaching across difference to participate in God's actions bringing justice and healing to our world in crisis'.

[3] Russel, *Just Hospitality*, p. 20.

[4] Russel, *Just Hospitality*, p. 65.

fear the possibility of the unknown and the prospect of being culturally 'contaminated' by their otherness, or even worse, being physically endangered by it. Therefore, hospitality is not natural – it is divine and supernatural. It is a gift of the Creator sharing Himself with His creature – of humanity becoming partaker in the divine nature, making its habitat in God and extending the hospitality of the divine communal life to the rest of the world. In His unconditional redeeming hospitality, God becomes home for humanity so that, in return, humanity may make the world into a home for all. Thus, hospitality is welcoming the stranger at home without imposing upon them the demand 'to fit' in our space. Scripture describes hospitality as work and gift of the Spirit – expression of the charismatic presence of God in and with His people on earth – the community of the saints – the embodied human form of the Trinitarian communal life.

In light of the above, the present chapter will offer a brief reflection on the event of Pentecost (the quintessential point of reference within Pentecostal theological inquiry) and the birth of Christ-like communal consciousness. The text will then discuss the significance of the language of the other and the demand for cosmopolitan hospitality engaging the work of Jacques Derrida and Emmanuel Levinas. It will further focus on the act of creation and the event of the Incarnation as expressions of the hospitality of God. The chapter will highlight the concern of the risks of hospitality and will discuss the Old Testament concept of 'the cities of refuge', the event of Pentecost, and the eschatological vision of the City of God as forms of public communal practice of the radical hospitality of God towards the other, incarnated in the community of faith via the agency of the Holy Spirit.

Pentecost and the Birth of Christ-like Communal Consciousness

The contemporary Western (or European) ideas of human rights, equality, and justice stand upon the foundations of the Judeo-Christian tradition and its ability to generate and sustain a covenantal communal consciousness.[5] This consciousness is induced by a vision of God whose identity and character are revealed in his continual preoccupation with justice for the other. Indeed, God places the other into the center of personal and corporate social redemption (Deut. 5.16-21; Exod. 20.12-17) and establishes the communal covenant as the immediate embodiment and extension of the salvific covenant. Those who stand in covenant with this God (the eternal proto-community of the Trinity) are called also to covenant with one another – prioritizing the well-being of the other by the spiritual discipline of fasting from oneself out of love for God and neighbor. The practice of this liturgical *askesis* forms the believers into the likeness of God.

As was already established in Chapter 1, attaining the likeness of God in Christ-likeness could be viewed as the ultimate calling and purpose of all humanity.[6] The realization of the divine likeness, demands one's continual transfiguring encompassing the sanctification of personal will and desires. Pentecost inaugurates the beginning of this Christoforming work of the Holy Spirit in the community of faith[7] by making it the dwelling place and embodied reality of the Trinitarian *koinonia* in the cosmos. The creature has been united with the Triune God and empowered by the Holy Spirit to live the likeness of the divine life within the material world.[8]

The Christic civic spirituality associated with the covenantal communal consciousness of the new humanity is further nurtured by an eschatological expectancy of the global spread of the Kingdom of God – until Christ's comprehensive justice covers the earth

---

[5] Max Stackhouse, 'Sources and Prospects for Human Rights Ideas: A Christian Perspective', in Jindřich Halama (ed.), *The Idea of Human Rights: Traditions and Presence* (Prague, Czech Republic: UK ETF, 2003), pp. 183-84.

[6] Christophoros Stavropoulos, 'Partakers of Divine Nature' in Daniel B. Clendenin (ed.), *Eastern Orthodox Theology: A Contemporary Reader* (Grand Rapids, MI: Baker Books, 1995), pp. 183-84. For an expounded account on Pentecost and the attaining the likeness of God, see Daniela C. Augustine, 'Pentecost, Empowerment and Glossolalia', *International Journal for the Study of the Christian Church* 11.4 (November 2011), pp. 288-304.

[7] Lossky, *Orthodox Theology: An Introduction*, p. 85.

[8] Therefore, as St. Basil asserts, the empowerment of the Holy Spirit is for 'perfection in holiness' as 'an unyielding, unchangeable commitment to goodness' – holiness as God-likeness that 'is impossible without the Spirit'. St. Basil the Great, *On the Holy Spirit* (Crestwood, NY: St. Vladimir's Seminary Press, 1980), p. 63.

as the waters of the sea. The ultimate vision of the world's destiny is its transfiguring into a house of prayer, worship, and healing in which all nations are bonded in a covenantal global community (Rev. 7.9-10). This cosmopolitan vision is sustained by a spirituality incarnated in the community of faith that lives out the reality of the Kingdom as a faith-praxis of the Body of Christ on behalf of the world.

As such, the Body represents a new Christ-like consciousness in the world. This consciousness of the Kingdom is expressed in a redemptive relationship with the other as love for God and neighbor (Mt. 27.37-40). Since Christ's messianic mission is fulfilled in self-giving to the other, the consciousness formed by the Spirit in His Body is an antidote to selfishness. While selfishness commodifies, consumes, marginalizes, and even eliminates the other for one's own benefit, the messianic consciousness of Christ's Body prioritizes the other's wellbeing.

The fact that Christ is the Truth (Jn 14.6) that sets people free (Jn 8.32) brings into view the image of the prophetic Pentecost community as a truth-embodying and truth-proclaiming social reality that unites the story of the Kingdom with its praxis. The community's voice in the life of the human *polis* calls all civic dimensions to moral responsibility and discernment between good and evil. Once again, the incarnation is essential for exercising discernment, for each spirit is known by its fruit (Mt. 7.16, 1 Jn 4.2), and the fruit of the Holy Spirit is revealed within the human *socium* precisely through the prioritization of the other as a beneficiary of the social capital produced in the believer's life by the Spirit's Christo-forming presence (Gal. 5.22-23).

This aspect of the Kingdom is an outcome of the Spirit's dialectic of liberation. This new human consciousness is not a result of social evolution (Hegel) or revolution (Marx). Rather, as Nicolas Berdyaev has stated, the Kingdom of God is an outcome of a 'marvelous transfiguration'.[9] Marx's saint and hero was Prometheus. He stole fire from the gods in order to give it to humanity and meet the human need of light, illumination, and the freedom to chart one's own journey. In contrast, the fire of the Spirit is a divine act of self-

[9] Nicolas Berdyaev, *Philosophy of Inequality* (Sofia: Prozoretz, 1923), p. 220.

giving, an expression of divine hospitality. In this fire a self-pouring God meets all human needs. God's Spirit invites humans into His light, gives them dreams and visions, and empowers them to prophesy a just socio-political reality beyond the order of empires. Herein lies a true actualization of human freedom in covenantal community with the Trinity and with one another. The light of the Spirit illuminates and initiates the dialectic of true human freedom beginning with clarity of vision – 'you shall know the truth and the truth shall set you free' (Jn 8.32). This is a different kind of knowing than that of the Marxist revolutionary consciousness emphasizing one's self-interest as a representative of the proletarian class. Illuminated by the Spirit, the liberating epistemology is that of knowing Christ in the other (Mt. 25.31-46) – or knowing otherwise.[10] First of all, knowing the truth is being in a covenant with the One Who is the Truth and then seeing Him in the other even in their 'most distressful disguise' (Mother Teresa). Knowing the Truth gives us His perspective towards the other, informing and constructing our actions. The other is known otherwise than in the homogenizing demands of imperial consciousness. We come to know the other as Christ knows him or her, a knowing in which human dignity and wholeness are restored. It is the knowing of love in flesh – knowing in Christ-likeness.

It is no accident that the language of the other stands at the center of the Pentecost event as an expression of the prioritization of the other in the Kingdom of the new humanity. As was noted in Chapter 1, Jean-François Lyotard reminds us that the translatability of language points to the fact that all human beings are called to a speech community and that the silencing of the speech of the other is a violation of a basic right.[11] Human speech is therefore inseparable from the notion of justice as 'the relationship to the other', and knowing the language of the other is integral to knowing the other's reality.

---

[10] James H. Olthuis (ed.), *Knowing Other-Wise: Philosophy at the Threshold of Spirituality* (New York: Fordham University Press, 1997), p. 8.

[11] J.-F. Lyotard, 'The Other's Rights', in S. Shute and S. Hurley (eds.), *On Human Rights* (New York: Basic Books, 1993), pp. 140-41.

The Language of the Other and the Demand for Cosmopolitan Hospitality

The seemingly uncontested claims of global capitalism and Western democratic theory over the world's cosmopolitan future have highlighted the problems of institutionalized multiculturalism within the current discourse on globalization.[12] Multiculturalism is suspect in evading the mandate to cultivate authentically dialogical spaces and in serving, instead, as a propaganda vehicle of Western capitalism. Seeing institutionalized multiculturalism as the universalizing force of global capitalism, Slavoj Zizek suggests that its current position in the world entails *Eurocentric* (or perhaps North-Atlantic) *distance*.[13] This distance outwardly displays an attitude of respect and tolerance toward the local cultures while insisting on its cultural superiority among them.[14] Its position of cultural relativism recognizes the voice of the other yet makes the other irrelevant to the economic and political mechanisms of global governance. The voice of the other is reduced to just one more parallel voice among many. The other has the right to exist as long as he or she does not dominate the development of the global political space. Therefore, Western multiculturalism assumes the position of a superior subject who, due to its neutrality, can be a universal representative and can exercise an uncontested global rule.[15] While accommodating polyphony within the boundaries of its convenience, institutionalized Western

---

[12] The tension between Western liberal democracy and multiculturalism is not new. For example, it is evident in the work of John Stuart Mill. While writing passionately in defense of individual freedom, Mill wholeheartedly supports the colonization policy of the British Empire. He believed that 'despotism is a legitimate mode of government in dealing with barbarians, provided the end be their improvement and the means justified by actually effecting the ends'. *On Liberty* (New York: Penguin Books, 1985), p. 11.

[13] Slavoj Zizek, 'Multiculturalism', p. 44.

[14] Yegenoglou, 'Liberal Multiculturalism and the Ethics of Hospitality in the Age of Globalization', *Postmodern Culture* (http://www3.iath.virginia.edu/pmc/issue.103/13.2yegenoglu.html).

[15] David Lloyd, in 'Race under Representation,' has articulated the concept of 'the subject with ultimate properties;' 'Its universality is attained by virtue of literal indifference: this subject becomes representative in consequence of being able to take anonymous place, of occupying any place, of pure exchangeability. Universal, where all others are particular, partial, this subject is perfect, disinterested judge formed for and by the public sphere'. *Oxford Literary Review* 13.1-2 (1991), pp. 70.

multiculturalism, through its insistence on relativity, effectively eliminates the need of a dialogue with the other. In a Bakhtinian sense, it asserts monological utterance over against the development of dialogical *heteroglossia.* Since language is a historically charged reality, dialogical unity with the other involves participation in the story of the other. However, this co-habitation of the story of the other provides, at the same time, an-other perspective on one's own language and story.[16] The individual is able to see his/herself through the eye of the other.

By relativizing the voice of the other, we eliminate the need for dialogical participation in and with the other. In this manner, institutionalized multiculturalism effectively obscures and belittles the significance of alternative voices. The elimination of the need for a dialogue compromises human sociality, connectivity, and community. It trivializes the covenantal social relationships that create authentically democratic space and secure the participation of the other in the formation of a cosmopolitan civil society. The absence of dialogue eliminates the inconvenience of the need to learn the language of the other. Consequently, it relieves us from the burden of recognizing the other *de facto,* even when it is required to recognize them *de jure.*

Engaging Zizek's reflection on Western multiculturalism, Mayda Yegenoglu poses the following critical question: 'If the institutionalized pluralism that characterizes the post-national global order implies a foreclosure of politics proper and is far from offering a potential for democratic politization, then where do we locate the possibility of politics that interrupt this foreclosure?'[17] In search of an answer to this question, Yegenoglu turns to Jacques Derrida's argument concerning conditional and unconditional hospitality as a useful 'apparatus for deconstructing the ideology imbedded in liber-

---

[16] M. Bakhtin, 'Response to a Question from Novy Mir Editorial Staff', in Caryl Emerson and Michael Holquist (eds.), *Speech Genres and Other Late Essays* (trans. Vern W. McGee; Austin, TX: The University of Texas, 1986), pp. 1-7. See also James P. Zappen, 'Mikhail Bakhtin', in Michael G. Morgan and Michelle Ballif (eds.), *Twentieth-Century Rhetoric and Rhetoricians: Critical Studies and Sources* (Westport: Greenwood Press, 2000), pp. 7-20.

[17] Yegenoglou, 'Liberal Multiculturalism', p. 6.

al multiculturalism'.[18] Deconstructing this ideology thus creates conditions for a 'democratic possibility' on a cosmopolitan scale.

Derrida contrasts Kant's cosmopolitical law as 'law or politics of hospitality' with Levinas' 'ethics of hospitality' while addressing the question of the possibility of both within the global human existence.[19] According to Derrida, rethinking Levinas' ethical discourse on hospitality invites us 'to think law and politics otherwise'; such rethinking could open 'both the mouth and the possibility of another speech'.[20] Derrida sees the relationship between conditional and unconditional hospitality in a manner similar to that between law and justice. The law can be deconstructed – it could be analyzed, critiqued, and changed. The history of legal systems is 'a history of the transformation of law'.[21] Conversely, Derrida clarifies that justice is not the law.

> Justice is what gives us the impulse, the drive, or the movement to improve the law ... Justice is not reducible to the law, to a given system of legal structures. That means that justice is always unequal to itself. It is non-coincidental with itself.[22]

Derrida embraces Levinas' definition of justice as being 'the relation to the other'[23] and points out the fact that in accordance with such an understanding, justice continually questions the law since it is always 'incalculable' and 'unequal to the other'.[24] In view of that,

---

[18] Yegenoglou, 'Liberal Multiculturalism', p. 16.

[19] Derrida's work on hospitality has occupied the text of various volumes; however, the immediate association with this topic brings us to the following two titles: *Adieu to Emmanuel Levinas* (Stanford, CA: Stanford University Press, 1990) and *Of Hospitality*, with parallel text by Anne Dufourmantelle (Stanford, CA: Stanford University Press, 2000). Derrida, *Adieu*, pp. 19-20. On the contrast between Kant and Levinas see also pp. 48-51.

[20] Derrida, *Adieu*, p. 21.

[21] Derrida, *Deconstruction in a Nutshell: A Conversation with Jacques Derrida* (ed. John D. Caputo; New York: Fordham University Press, 1997), p. 16. The first chapter of the book records the Villanova Roundtable conversation with Derrida.

[22] Derrida, *Deconstruction in a Nutshell*, p. 16. See also Derrida, 'The Force of Law: 'The Mystical Foundation of Authority' in Drucilla Cornell *et al.*, *Deconstruction and the Possibility of Justice* (trans. Mary Quaintance; New York: Routledge, 1992), pp. 68-91 in, pp. 14-15.

[23] Levinas, *Totality and Infinity* (trans. Alphonso Lingis; Pittsburgh: Duquesne University Press, 1969), p. 89.

[24] Derrida, *Deconstruction in a Nutshell*, p. 17. In understanding Derrida's idea of *justice,* it is helpful to also look at the idea of *the gift*. See Derrida's *The Gift of Death*

Derrida invites us 'to think of another way of interpreting politics' as 'the place for hospitality, the place for the gift',[25] and to rethink 'the concepts of the political and of democracy' in a way that would be compatible and articulated with 'these impossible notions of the gift and justice'.[26]

Derrida points out that legislated hospitality is conditional. It subjugates the guest (the stranger, the foreigner) to the law of one's home. Therefore, it allows the stranger to enter the hosts' space under the hosts' conditions and regulations.[27] Reflecting on Kant's *categorical imperative,* Derrida suggests that

> to be what it 'must' be, hospitality must not pay a debt, or be governed by a duty: ... unconditional law of hospitality, if such thing is thinkable, would then be a law without imperative, without order and without duty. A law without law in short.[28]

The language of the other is of great significance in Derrida's and Levinas' understanding of hospitality. According to Levinas, 'the essence of language is goodness ... is friendship and hospitality'.[29] Hospitality is 'interrupting oneself' in opening space for the other,[30] or welcoming the other. Therefore, hospitality is 'intentionality, consciousness of, attention to speech or welcome of the face' of the other.[31]

In his discourse on hospitality, Derrida makes the important observation that: 'Language resists all mobilities because it moves about' with us.[32] Therefore, displaced people – 'exiles, the deported, the expelled, the rootless, the stateless, lawless nomads, absolute foreigners, often continue to recognize the language, what is called

---

(trans. David Wills; Chicago: University of Chicago Press, 1995), and *Given Time: I. Counterfeit Money* (trans. Peggy Kamuf; Chicago: University of Chicago Press, 1991). Regarding justice and the other is helpful to see Levinas' discourse on 'the Face'. Levinas, *Totality and Infinity*, p. 229.

25 Derrida, *Deconstruction in a Nutshell*, p. 18.

26 Derrida, *Deconstruction in a Nutshell*, p. 19.

27 Derrida, *Of Hospitality*, pp. 75-85.

28 Derrida, *Of Hospitality*, p. 83.

29 Levinas, *Totality and Infinity*, p. 305.

30 Derrida, *Adieu*, pp. 52-53.

31 Levinas, *Totality and Infinity*, p. 299.

32 Derrida, *Of Hospitality*, p. 91.

the mother tongue, as their ultimate homeland, and even their last resting place'.[33]

If the mother-tongue is our mobile habitat – our home away from home, then it is essential to the act of welcoming the other in unconditional hospitality. When the other encounters their mother-tongue in us, they enter their homeland. Our space becomes their space, and they are finally at home.

Discussing the possibility and impossibility of unconditional hospitality, Derrida gives the final word to Levinas and his Torah-inspired stand for the other as the focal point of all ethics. Levinas states:

> The Torah is transcendent and from heaven by its demands that clash, in the final analysis, with the pure ontology of the world. The Torah demands, in opposition to the natural perseverance of each being in his or her own being (a fundamental ontological law), concern for the stranger, the widow and the orphan, a pre-occupation with the other person.[34]

Derrida ends his *Adieu to Emmanuel Levinas* with this quote, thus fulfilling the mandate of the very subject of the book. He fittingly adopts the language of Levinas in a final gesture of farewell and parting gift of hospitality to his late colleague.

Creation, Incarnation, and the Hospitality of God

In his book, *The Trinity and the Kingdom*, Jürgen Moltmann offers a compelling image of God as Creator epitomizing the essence of divine love. This is the image of God's 'withdrawal of himself', his 'self-limitation' in opening space for the existence of creation.[35] This image is a profound expression of the Trinity (itself an act of love) and could be considered as the *motherhood* of God and therefore as hospitality *par excellence*. The reflexive re-spacing of the Creator as a cosmic womb that conceives, tabernacles, nurtures, and

---

[33] Derrida, *Of Hospitality*, pp. 87, 89.

[34] Levinas, *In the Time of the Nations* (trans. Michael B. Smith; London: The Atholone Press, 1994), p. 61. Derrida ends with this passage his book *Adieu to Emmanuel Levinas*.

[35] Jürgen Moltmann, *The Trinity and the Kingdom* (Minneapolis, MN: Fortress Press, 1993), p. 59.

sustains the other is consistent with God's continual self-giving in his relation to humanity and the rest of creation. A womb symbolizes sanctuary and self-sacrifice. A womb embraces one's irreversible transfiguring, for it is motivated by love that is committed to birth forth life – the life of the other. It is a gift of unconditional hospitality.[36] God becomes the immediate dwelling place of the other as the very environment in which they live and move and have their being (Acts 17.28).

In the first chapter of Genesis we see God creating within the divine communal self not only a sanctuary for the possibility and flourishing of the other but also building a home for them.[37] He takes time in carefully crafting and furnishing this home according to the physical needs of his creatures so that they may truly have access to life more abundant. He personally dwells there with them (Gen. 3.8) providing not only a shelter and material sustenance but also fellowship in communal belonging. Thus, God meets the distinct human need of sociality, for a human life without community of unconditional acceptance is not life to the fullest; it is not life abundant for those created in the image of God. Yet, Scripture asserts that because the earth is not just any dwelling place but home in the presence of God, all creatures depend on the generous unconditional hospitality of the Creator whose providential care sustains their very life (Job 12.10, 34.14-15, Mt. 6.26, Lk. 12.24-28, Acts 17.25).

The unconditional hospitality of God in the act of creation culminates in the establishing of the Sabbath as a day of rest. Time is both an outcome of creation and the canvas on which God spreads the universe. Therefore, John Dominic Crossan invites us to consider:

> It is not humanity on the sixth day but the Sabbath on the seventh day that is the climax of creation. And therefore our 'do-

---

[36] While gendering religion can be problematic, the feminine experience of motherhood may provide a helpful lens towards grasping and articulating God's self-limitation on behalf of the other in the act of creation.

[37] For an exposition on God as an architect building and furnishing a house see John Dominic Crossan, *God and Empire: Jesus Against Rome, Then and Now* (New York: Harper One, 2007), pp. 51-52.

minion' over the world is not ownership but stewardship under the God of the Sabbath.[38]

Thus, the seventh day is a day of rest for all of God's creatures. This is the day in which God gives humanity relief from its labor and commands it to do likewise to the other. Both the anthropic and the non-anthropic creation is to enjoy the unconditional care of God in the Sabbath rest, a gesture of all-encompassing cosmic hospitality provided by the divine host for His creatures. Yet, as we have already seen, hospitality is justice and the recipients of the divine welcome are to extend it to others as an act of 'God's own distributive justice'.[39] Therefore, Sabbath rest is commanded for one's entire household and all of his/her dependents – sons and daughters, male and female servants, farm animals and livestock. The Sabbath is justice as radical equality from which even the resident alien who lives in Israel is not exempted (Deut. 5.14). The Sabbath logic as all-comprehensive justice of divine hospitality is further translated into the Sabbath Year and the Sabbath Jubilee. This is not just 'rest *for* worship but rest *as* worship'[40] in recognition of the ownership of God upon all of creation, including time, and of the creatures' full dependence on the divine grace as hospitality.

In the act of creation, God gives the world to humanity in self-sharing as a gift of life in substance and beauty so that humanity may, in turn, learn to share it with the other and the different. The world is a gift with a pedagogical function – helping humanity 'to grow spiritually'[41] – to grow in the likeness of God. This pedagogy develops through the 'dialogue of the gift' that brings God and humanity together in the gesture of self-sacrificial giving.[42] Since humanity does not have anything of its own to give to God, it learns to give back to the Creator from the Creation (e.g. the tithe, the Sabbath). The greatest gift in this exchange is that of giving one-self, giving one's own life.[43] This is also the ultimate call to the

---

[38] Crossan, *God and Empire*, p. 53.

[39] Crossan, *God and Empire*, p. 54.

[40] Crossan, *God and Empire*, p. 54.

[41] Staniloae, *The Experience of God*, p. 22.

[42] Staniloae, *The Experience of God*, p. 22.

[43] Staniloae writes, 'The paradox [of the return of the gift] is explained by the fact that the gift received and returned draws the persons close to one another to such an extent that the object of the gift becomes something common and comes

likeness of God for humanity communicated in God's self-giving in Christ.

In the act of creation, God establishes his self-limitation on behalf of the other. This is an act of fasting from oneself in order to nurture the other that becomes paradigmatic for one's striving towards attaining the likeness of God. Therefore, being holy as God is holy (1 Pet. 1.15-16) includes unconditional covenantal love towards the other as one's neighbor (Eph. 1.4). This is why the Decalogue delineates the conditions of holiness in the likeness of God while establishing the social covenant (commandments six through ten) as part of the fulfillment of the divine covenant (Exod. 20.1-17). In this mandate for justice towards the other we see the manifestation of the paradox of unconditional hospitality in which the host has to submit (in Derrida's terms) to the conditions of the guest – the host and the guest have to exchange roles in the same household. Thus, one has to welcome the socio-political reality of the justice of God as justice for the other in order, in return, to be welcomed by God in His redeeming justice of forgiveness and unconditional acceptance.

This paradox of unconditional hospitality is also evident in the event of the Incarnation. In the Incarnation, we see Christ as both guest and host, recipient and giver of divine hospitality. God's embodied entry into the world is tangibly embraced in the unconditional hospitality of Mary in whose womb He tabernacles, becoming flesh and dwelling among us. He receives Mary and Joseph's parental care – also unconditional hospitality – as their family relationships are re-spaced in order to include the Son of God. As His earthly parents, they provide all they can for His needs through a selfless love that welcomes this ultimate stranger and gives itself fully to Him. This is hospitality as love and love as a sanctuary.

In the Incarnation, creation welcomes the Creator and becomes its home. Matter welcomes the Spirit in truly unconditional hospi-

---

to be the transparent means for the fullest communion between persons. And not only is the gift something common, but it is also increased through the life which the persons communicate to one another through the love manifested in the gift they make; in this way the persons give themselves as a gift, and through this giving they grow spiritually' (*The Experience of God*, p. 22); and 'The dialogue of the gift between God and the human person lies in the fact that each bestows himself upon the other' (*The Experience of God*, p. 23).

tality in which the host submits to the terms of the guest. Matter allows the Spirit to take it upon itself and reshape it according to the divine will and purpose. This is matter embracing the mystery of the full divinity and humanity of the Son of God. Matter becomes sanctuary for the Incarnated God so that He in turn may become a sanctuary for matter. For indeed, in the Incarnation matter meets the redemptive embrace of divine hospitality, as its elemental structure and content are welcomed into the inner-circle of the Trinitarian communal life through the body of the Son. The eternal Word that spoke matter into existence reunites with matter so that the ontological relation between Creator and Creation may be redeemed in the eschatological reality of the Cosmic Christ. As Alexander Schmemann asserts, 'In the world of incarnation nothing neutral remains, nothing can be taken away from the Son of man'.[44] In the Incarnation, 'the great scandal of metaphysics',[45] matter is sanctified and sanctioned as an instrument of grace in the consecration of the cosmos.

Therefore, the Incarnation is a powerful anti-Gnostic statement, affirming the goodness and innocence of matter, victimized through the violent consequences of the Fall of humanity. The conditions of the curse have antagonized matter as a part of creation torn by and infused with violence against the other.[46] The first Adam is responsible for the curse that permeated creation and caused its consequent suffering and distortion. The last Adam – Jesus Christ – sets free from the curse not only humanity, but also the rest of creation. Creation anticipates this redemption at the birth of the Savior and celebrates together with heaven the grace of God in the mystery of the Incarnation. Those who are present hear angelic choirs and see heavenly fireworks – a 'traveling' supernova followed by wise men making their pilgrimage to the New-born King (Mt. 2.1-2, 9-11). Poor shepherds and their flocks witness the

---

44 Alexander Schmemann, 'The Missionary Imperative', p. 201.

45 Lossky, *Orthodox Theology: An Introduction*, p. 91.

46 In Gen. 3.14-19 the articulation of the curse outlines this all permeating violent conflict with the other in the struggle of the woman against nature in the pain of childbearing, the man against the woman in fight for domination, the man against nature in the resistance of the earth to give him the fruit of his labor, one creature against another in the battle between the woman's seed and the snake.

cosmic event that unites haven and earth in the fragile body of an infant (Lk. 2.8-20). The cosmos welcomes the Creator in anticipation of its own welcome into life eternal.

Through the Incarnation, matter participates in the drama of redemption and its culmination in the Passion of the Christ. Thus, in His broken, crucified body matter is subjugated to torture and death so that it may overcome death. In the last Adam matter's innocence is met with the moral purity of the Son of Man who, while tempted in all things, still remains without sin (Heb. 1.15). Thus, death has no power over Him and His material body. His incarnation, crucifixion, and resurrection overcome the consequences of humanity's fall and exhaust the power of sin and death (1 Cor. 15.26).[47] Thus, the triumph of redemption culminates in the resurrection in which the Spirit welcomes matter out of death into eternal life. Matter's possibility of life in eternity is contingent on divine hospitality for only God is eternal (non-contingent, without beginning and end). Thus, matter experiences eternity only as a gift of divine welcome in which God shares His life with the other so that they may have life eternal.

The earthly ministry of Jesus, the incarnated eternal Logos, also underlines the paradox of unconditional hospitality (of the inversion of host and guest) evident in the dialectic of the spread of the Kingdom of God. As humanity welcomes the King, He, in return, welcomes humanity into His Kingdom. The Kingdom is seeded on earth as the smallest seed in the garden but when it falls in a good/hospitable ground it outgrows everything else and translates the world into the loving embrace of unconditional divine hospitality (Mk 4.30-32).

Through the Incarnation of the eternal Logos, Jesus Christ becomes Scripture applied to the totality of human life with its all-encompassing social relationships. He is the in-fleshed application and fulfillment of the Law and the Prophets and their mandate for unconditional hospitality as justice for the other. He alone is/has the 'words of eternal life' (Jn 6.68) needed to redeem and restore human inter-sociality and transfigure it into an embodiment of the

---

[47] Christophoros Stavropoulos, 'Partakers of Divine Nature', in Daniel B. Clendenin (ed.), *Eastern Orthodox Theology: A Contemporary Reader* (Grand Rapids, MI: Baker Books, 1995), p. 188.

divine likeness (of the Triune communal life) into human society as radical equality, freedom, and justice for all. Among this all-encompassing self-application of the Incarnated Word to human life, the Gospels highlight Christ's powerful authoritative reinterpretations of the law's prescribed relationships to strangers, Gentiles, women, children, the poor, the oppressed, the marginalized, the excluded. They all enjoy unconditional divine hospitality in His acts of benevolence as healing, forgiveness, acceptance, and inclusion. They are all welcomed into the Kingdom of God and experience its advent within their own life as redemption, restoration, wholeness, and community. As Jesus visits the homes of sinners and fellowships with tax collectors, prostitutes, and Gentiles, salvation comes to their households (Lk. 19.1-10) – they welcome the Kingdom and in return are welcomed by it.[48] God makes them part of His household and seats them around His table making them beneficiaries of the divine hospitality – He becomes their home.

This practice of divine hospitality extended by God in Christ becomes the mandate for His Body, the Church. She is to become, in Christ-likeness, a sanctuary for the other and the different. As Amos Yong reminds us, the 'trinitarian logic that entails God as Giver, Given, and Giving – a truly perichoretic hospitality – initiates, sustains, and solicits, rather than requires, by law or otherwise, our own giving'.[49] Yong argues that since Christians are aliens and strangers in this world they are perpetual guests who should view themselves as recipients of hospitality 'first from God and then from others' even when they find themselves as hosts.[50] Christine D. Pohl asserts that hospitality to the alien, to the stranger, and to the marginalized is best practiced by those who 'have a sense of their own alien status'.[51] She argues that

> The most transformative expressions of hospitality, both historically and in our own time, are associated with hosts who are lim-

[48] Regarding Jesus as a recipient of hospitality in the accounts of Luke–Acts, see Amos Yong, *Hospitality and the Other: Pentecost, Christian Practices, and the Neighbor* (Maryknoll, NY: Orbis Books, 2008), pp. 100-103.

[49] Yong, *Hospitality and the Other*, p. 127.

[50] Yong, *Hospitality and the Other*, p. 124-25.

[51] Christine D. Pohl, *Making Room: Recovering Hospitality as a Christian Tradition* (Grand Rapids, MI: Eerdmans, 1999), p. 124.

> inal, marginal, or at the lower end of the social order. These hosts are essentially threshold or bridge people, connected in some ways to the larger society but distinct from it either in actual social situation or in self-imposed distance. Without these crucial dimensions of marginality and liminality, the relations between hosts and guests often serve the more conservative function of reinforcing existing social relations and status hierarchies.[52]

Pohl reflects on the fact that, consistent with the awareness of their own marginality, the poor and the dispossessed are often more willing to share their limited resources with the needy, thus pointing to the possibility of an inverse relation between wealth and hospitality.[53] Indeed, when one practices hospitality not out of a position of ownership but of stewardship of his/her home and possessions, their hospitality is transformed into a gift from God of which both the hosts and the guests are equal recipients. Ultimately, it is the hospitality of God that is offered and received by the other through the agency of the Holy Spirit.

The Risk of Hospitality

Unconditional hospitality implies some potential dangers and risks. We are afraid that the other can be abusive of our hospitality, that he/she may rob our possessions or take over our home.[54] We are afraid of the potential violence the other may bring into our world, endangering not only our wellbeing, but also our very lives. Thus, we meet strangers with suspicion and worry. We make sure that a safe distance is kept between us and them at all times. If, in addition to socio-economic status, their strangeness encompasses cultural

---

[52] Pohl, *Making Room* , pp. 106-107.

[53] Pohl provides extensive reflection in support of this claim. Pohl, *Making Room*, pp. 114-19, pp. 123-24. Perhaps this inverse relation is evident in the warm reception and hospitality shown by the social outcasts and the marginalized to Jesus and His teaching, but also in the story of the poor widow giving all that she has as a love-offering in the temple (Mk 12.42-44) or the story of the rich young ruler who departs empty-handed and disappointed while Jesus' words affirm the impossibility of the rich entering the Kingdom of heaven (Mt. 19.16-24).

[54] For more on concrete risks pertaining to the practice of hospitality see Pohl, *Making Room*, pp. 85-89.

otherness of religion, ethnicity or race, the distance between us becomes even harder to bridge. Therefore, our perplexed and anxious social imagination is capable of casting every Muslim as a potential terrorist, every Christian from another tradition as a superstitious and ignorant idolater, every ethnically other as an illegal alien – a criminal intruder who is after our jobs, prosperity, and safety.

In addressing the issue of the risks of unconditional hospitality while faced with the need to protect our homes and communities when extending welcome to absolute strangers, Christine D. Pohl points out that hospitality 'begins at the gate, in the doorway, on the bridges between public and private space'.[55] Therefore, threshold communities whose members understand both the world of the guest and that of the host culture are very important in welcoming the stranger in our midst. The Church is meant to be such a threshold community of welcome for the other.

While public policy on immigrants and refugees attempts to provide a safety protocol that differentiates between the ill-willed and dangerous intruder and the one in true need of sanctuary, its institutions function as defense-systems, as gate-keepers and not as agents of benevolent hospitality. Therefore, it is not surprising that they often display a politically-prescribed myopia towards the other's existential needs, pronouncing them illegitimate and insignificant. After all, we see state politics being preoccupied with 'control of immigration' and not with providing humanitarian solutions to refugee demands even when their very survival depends on finding political or economic asylum.[56] The state immigration laws commonly display the conflict of interest between the law of (conditional) hospitality and the ethic of (unconditional) hospitality, or rather ethic as hospitality.[57]

The Church, conversely, is free from the restrictions of legislated hospitality to the stranger and can function as a true public welcom-

---

[55] Pohl, *Making Room*, p. 95.

[56] Derrida expounds on the conflict between politics of hospitality and ethics of hospitality pointing to the preoccupation of politics with control of immigration versus solving the humanitarian problems of refugees (Derrida, *On Cosmopolitanism and Forgiveness*, pp. 12-16).

[57] Derrida objects against the use of the term 'ethic of hospitality' stating that hospitality 'is culture itself and not simply one ethic amongst others' (*On Cosmopolitanism and Forgiveness*, p. 16).

ing community on the threshold between cultural, linguistic, economic, ethnic, and racial divides. The Church – herself a community of aliens, strangers, and pilgrims from every tongue and nation – is a continual recipient of the hospitality of God and her cultural marginality delineates her status as both the guest and host of the Kingdom in the midst of alternative socio-political contexts of this world. Therefore, in the moment in which the Church assumes the position of cultural representation on behalf of the broader host culture, she counterfeits her prophetic identity of a public threshold community (where the human city enters the City of God) and ceases to exist as an extension of God's divine hospitality in the world. The Church surrenders her identity as a place of refuge and a sanctuary of unconditional welcome for the other.

The Community of Faith as a Public Expression of Divine Hospitality

The Cities of Refuge

In the 1990s, the work of Jacques Derrida and Emmanuel Levinas stirred up the cosmopolitical imagination of the global village by recapturing a particular Old Testament expression of divine hospitality as distributive justice for the other enacted through the community of faith. In highlighting the need of rethinking cosmopolitanism in terms of renewal of international immigration and refugee laws and challenging the conventional politics of the liberal state, Derrida insists on reclaiming and adapting the role of the ancient 'cities of refuge' as 'a memorable heritage' and 'an original concept' of the duty of and right to hospitality.[58] The idea of the 'cities of refuge' is especially relevant to concerns about the dangers and risks of hospitality in finding a solution within the public domain that upholds justice for both the one who seeks and the one who offers refuge. What is the origin of this inspiration?

According to Numbers 35, God gives instruction to Moses to establish six cities of refuge (three on each side of the river Jordan) and to give them to the Levites (v. 6) who are to be their core citizens and caretakers. These cities are the places (ordained by divine

---

58 Derrida, *On Cosmopolitanism and Forgiveness*, p. 5.

justice) where an unintentional manslayer, an Israelite, an alien, or sojourner (v. 15) can flee and find refuge from the 'avenger of blood'. If a person kills a fellow human unintentionally, due to negligence leading to an accident (e.g. if an axe-head flies off the handle and kills someone), they can find sanctuary in one of these cities. The person still pays a price for his/her negligence – they go into exile, yet, their life is spared and protected. In fact, the congregation of God's people who have judged the manslayer and pronounced him innocent are obligated to 'deliver the manslayer from the blood avenger' and to 'restore him to his city of refuge where he fled', where 'he shall live … until the death of the high priest' (v. 25).

The justice of God mandates that the innocent manslayer should not be separated from human society. He is not to be exiled in the wilderness, but in a city populated with a flourishing community. In his reflections on the 'cities of refuge', Emmanuel Levinas utilizes an extensive excerpt from the Talmud (the Tractate Makkoth 10a). The text discusses all the special provisions that the Torah makes in the 'cities of refuge' for the one who seeks sanctuary and highlights a question posed by Rabbi Isaac: 'What is the scriptural authority (for all these provisions)?' The answer given by the Rabbi is: 'The verse: *and that fleeing unto one of these cities he might live* (Deuteronomy 4: 42) which means – provide him with whatever he needs so that he may [truly] live'.[59]

Thus, the Talmud instructs that if the population of a given city of refuge decreases, more people have to be relocated there. The text underlines that the Torah makes explicit provisions for the refugee: the city has to be located near water and pasture lands, and be able to provide food, shelter, functioning human community, and a sanctuary against the 'avenger of blood' so that innocent manslayers may live a normal life, so that their sociality may be intact and they may not be deprived from anything needed for their wellbeing, that they may not be dehumanized but may truly live.[60] In fact, the cities are given to the Levites so that the divine law may be taught and justice may be enacted on behalf of all its citizens. After all, the Torah is not just a cultural reality and its study is not a mere activity of

---

[59] Emmanuel Levinas, *Beyond the Verse: Talmudic Readings and Lectures* (London: Continuum, 2007), p. 34.

[60] Levinas, *Beyond the Verse*, pp. 34-36.

cultural transmission. The Torah is life and, therefore, it is the ultimate 'city of refuge' for it 'is stronger than death'.[61] In the city of refuge, God creates for the manslayer a place of true justice by providing what is needed for his/her flourishing.

The city of refuge is a place where the justice of God has provided access to life for the innocent, yet has kept them responsible for their negligence. The place is both a place of exile[62] and a sanctuary – it is a place of justice, forgiveness, and embrace where the people of God are to provide a healing community for the broken relationship between a person and his/her neighbor – putting an end to the cycle of violence induced by the thirst for revenge – a provision of social restoration and *shalom*.

In the middle ages, the churches and the monasteries occasionally took upon themselves the function of the cities of refuge. There the Christian community was to provide sanctuary to the unintentional manslayer and the wrongly accused, as well as to the political refugee so that they might be recipients of true justice.[63] Therefore, as in the cities of refuge so also in the Church, the people of God were to function as a public threshold community of welcome which took the risks of the practice of hospitality as justice for the stranger not only in recognition of duty (obligation) but as an expression of identity (ethic). The Church is to be the city on a hill where heaven descends on earth and makes its residence in humanity, saturating it with redemptive justice as love for God and neighbor. Therefore, it is not accidental that the rabbinical teaching on the cities of refuge ends with leaving the reader at 'Jerusalem as the gate of heaven'.[64] Levinas asserts that the symbolism of the text points to the impossibility for Israel (for the people of God, for the Church) to attain 'religious salvation without justice in the earthly city. No vertical dimension without a horizontal dimension ...

---

61 Levinas, *Beyond the Verse*, p. 45.

62 Levinas, *Beyond the Verse*, p. 42. Commenting on the response of Rabbi Issac, Levinas remarks: 'Life can thus mean only life worthy of the name; life in the full sense of the term: exile, of course, but not prison, no hard labour, and no concentration camp. Life which is life. The humanism or humanitarianism of the cities of refuge!'

63 Derrida, *On Cosmopolitanism and Forgiveness*, p. 18.

64 Levinas, *Beyond the Verse*, p. 38.

There is no other access to salvation than that which passes through the dwelling place' of humanity.[65]

The idea of sanctuary points to the fact that justice is more than doing what is right – it is repairing what is wrong, healing what is broken and making it whole; it is restoring access to life and life more abundant. Such a restoration is impossible without forgiveness and reconciliation with God and neighbor. This is why the justice of God is not satisfied with punishing humanity for its sins. In Christ, the embodied culmination and fullness of divine hospitality as comprehensive justice, God provides redemption from sin and victory over death (the consequence of sin) – He provides access to life eternal. The community of faith as the Body of Christ on earth and therefore, as a living extension of the resurrected Savior in the midst of a broken, destitute, and alienated world is called to do likewise. It is called to live out the justice of God on behalf of the world so that it may be healed and made whole. This redeeming justice starts with the household of God so that the entire world may become His household – so that the entire cosmos may become a sanctuary.

The Event of Pentecost

The event of Pentecost offers a paradigmatic vision of the incarnation of God's self-giving hospitality in the community of the believers as an extension of Christ's Body on earth. The outpouring of the Spirit upon the Body manifests God's self-sharing in welcoming all nations under heaven (Acts 2.5), through submitting His Word to the form and sound of their ethnic tongues (v. 6). Therefore, the proclamation speech of the faith community on the day of Pentecost embraces the language of the other. The divine embrace is no mere rhetorical strategy. It is a gift of divine hospitality. The Spirit invites all humanity to make its habitat in the inter-sociality of the Trinity. This invitation implies the host's self-giving (or surrender) to the other and not their colonization. It is an initiation of dialogue by re-spacing oneself and creating conditions for conversational inclusion of the other. It is a gesture of welcoming all foreigners, aliens, and strangers literally in their own terms.

---

[65] Levinas, *Beyond the Verse*, p. 38.

The all-inclusive multiplicity of languages employed by the Spirit in sharing the Good News about 'the mighty deeds of God' (v. 11) on behalf of all humanity brings together two significant dimensions of the divine hospitality. On the one hand, it demonstrates a differentiation among the ethnic groups within the multitude and pays attention to the unique singularities present within such diversity. On the other hand, the multiplicity of languages also expresses an affirmation of each separate ethnic identity and establishes the equality of each one before and in the presence of the Creator.

Therefore, the self-expression of God's Word in all ethnic tongues could also be viewed as their consecration. The Word fills the words of the nations with the story of God and translates itself into all languages while sustaining their unique distinctions. The languages of the people become the vocal embodiment of God's active, creative presence. The invitation to the people to embrace a common spiritual genesis and destiny does not eliminate but sustains ethnic diversity. The divine Word reminds the hearers that among humanity (in the words of Desmond Tutu) 'God has no enemies, only family'.[66]

On the day of Pentecost, the diverse multitude within the empire hears the Word of God, each in his/her own tongue. Among the hearers are those who have become displaced and dislocated as a result of the rise and fall of empires. As the Spirit brings the Word of God to them in the form and sound of their mother-tongue, the one non-transitional and immutable eternal reality that 'will never pass away' (Mt. 24.35) visits them in their mutability and displacement. As it indwells the mother-tongue, the Word of God welcomes them as a motherland in which they can find rest from their wandering and uncertainty of belonging. God becomes their eternal home, an act consistent with who He is in His self-giving from before the foundations of the world (1 Pet. 1.20).

The radical hospitality of God is further articulated in the vision of the prophesying community of faith (Acts 2.17-18). It is a vision of the future of the world as God's future. He invites and empowers humanity to speak forth its reality and content. The voices of the Spirit-saturated believers shape and form God's future for hu-

---

[66] Desmond Tutu, *God Has a Dream: A Vision of Hope for Our Time* (New York: Doubleday, 2004), p. 47.

manity by calling forth in prophetic utterance. The speakers and the Word become one incarnated creative force. This is a striking vision of the democratization of society, one in which radical emancipation and inclusivity permeate all socio-economic strata. Sons and daughters, old and young, bond slaves and free persons join their voices in speaking forth the just future of God. They all participate in the envisioning, articulation, and realization of that future. In a self-consistent act of hospitality, God grants them ownership of His future where He is all in all. In the Spirit, they extend the hospitality of God to the other and the different (to the class-opponent, to the demographically opposite) by embracing them as a part of their own destiny. Because the Spirit mandates the Body with the ministry of reconciliation (2 Cor. 5.18-19), the future becomes impossible without the voice of the other, including the enemy.[67] Therefore, global democracy becomes an outcome of divine hospitality taking residence in a Spirit-infused humanity.

It is the very nature of a Triune God to welcome the stranger, the wanderer, the marginalized, and the displaced in an embrace of divine hospitality. The Spirit – the great giver of dreams and visions – empowers the believers to prophesy together (in spite of their differences) and to imagine God's just future. This future is not a matter of speculation. It is incarnated by the Spirit in the Pentecost community in that community's identification with Christ as the *telos* of all existence. Therefore, the community of Pentecost enters the present from the future of the world as the realization of its social destiny and embraces it in the hospitality of God, transfiguring the human village into the City of God. In divine hospitality believers find belonging and community, and this is a hopeful discovery for a world traumatized in its global compression and exhausted political imagination. It is a hope for a future of cosmopolitan hospitality – the future of humanity in the likeness of God.

The City of God

The vision of the transformation of the world into a sanctuary is nowhere better articulated than in the book of Revelation and its

---

[67] In his book, *No Future without Forgiveness* (New York: Doubleday, 1999), pp. 257-63, Desmond Tutu offers a reflection out of the African context of ethnic conflicts, genocide, and apartheid. He points to the impossibility of societal future apart from forgiveness of the ones identified as enemies.

depiction of the City of God (Revelation 21). The reality of the Incarnation has brought the totality of human existence into the redemptive embrace of the Trinity. Even the city, this iconic quintessentially human project that spatially condenses and compresses human sociality (intensifying human relationships by squeezing them in closer proximity within the special enclosure of urban life) is brought into the infinite vastness of the proto-community of the Trinity. In the divine communal hospitality, the human city is faced with its ultimate transfiguration as it is welcomed within God's vision of the world's future. Thus, God's future for the world acquires a familiar human form – not a new Eden, but a New Jerusalem descends from heaven at the end of history as the polis of God becomes the polis of humanity. The socio-political reality of God's Kingdom enters the world not as a new garden but as a new city. This is a radical gesture of unconditional hospitality in which God subjects the reality of His future to the form of human civilization. Apart from this eschatological openness of divine hospitality, the comprehensive redemption of humanity will be impossible (after all, human civilization is indispensable to the reality of being human). As in the Incarnation, so in the final global advent of His Kingdom, God is not afraid that He may be contaminated by what is human. He takes upon Himself the totality of humanness in order to redeem it.

The City of God descends on earth as the bride of the Lamb, the community of the saints – the church of the redeemed (Rev. 21.2). As John Christopher Thomas observes in his marvelous commentary on the book of Revelation, 'The holy city and the holy people are one and the same'.[68] The Church is the City of God and she is filled with His glory (vv. 10-11) – His glory shines through her into the world. Therefore, the walls of the City are transparent so that nothing can obstruct the all-permeating light of the divine presence (v. 18). She is luminous with it, for the believers have become like their God and He is all in all within them (v. 23).

---

[68] John Christopher Thomas, *The Apocalypse: A Literary and Theological Commentary* (Cleveland, TN: CPT Press, 2012), p. 645. I am deeply indebted to Professor Thomas' insights in highlighting the symbolic meanings of the complex depiction of the City of God in Revelation 21.

The city has no temple (v. 22), in fact, as Thomas asserts, the entire city is a temple.[69] This is why the text describes its gates beginning with the Eastern one, according to the orientation of the city which is identical with the orientation of the temple in the old Jerusalem (1 Kgs 6.20). In fact, its length, width, and height are the same (v. 16) – the city is in the form of a cube like the Holy of Holies in the Jerusalem temple. The entire city is Holy of Holies.[70] It is a sanctuary in the very presence of God where unceasing worship takes place as all-comprehensive justice – the justice of God lived out daily by the community of faith as the communal embodiment of the divine life on earth (the life of the proto-community of the Trinity in-fleshed in the redeemed human society).

The magnitude of the city is breathtaking. Its size is unprecedented. It is beyond human comprehension – a mega-polis that, in the words of Thomas, stretches 'across the known world and into the heavens itself, perhaps indicating that the New Heaven and the New Earth unite in the New Jerusalem!'[71] The city of God has become the global village. The glory of God has covered the earth 'as the waters cover the sea' (Hab. 2.14).

The earth has been transformed into a sanctuary for all of God's creatures so that they may truly live. The believers as the temple of God on earth are now the very content of the heavenly city. God has become one with His people; Christ has become all in all and the Church herself has become the Holy of Holies of the world as an embodiment of absolute divine hospitality in the very presence of God. A sanctuary that has covered the globe – this is the Church in her *theosis*. This transfiguring journey that has started on the day of Pentecost has brought her to the summation of all existence into the likeness of Christ – it has consumed her beyond time into eternity.

---

[69] Thomas, *The Apocalypse*, p. 646.
[70] Thomas, *The Apocalypse*, p. 646.
[71] Thomas, *The Apocalypse*, p. 645.

Instead of Conclusion: From Pentecostalism to Pentecost as the Practice of Divine Hospitality in the Global Village

Contemporary institutionalized multiculturalism often asserts the transatlantic West as the host who determines the conditions of hospitality to the other in the planetary household. This assertion keeps the global South in the dependent position of being a perpetual guest and a mere recipient of the West's hospitality, thus being denied the right to feel truly at home in the global village. This is a disempowering experience[72] that keeps the other 'in their place' while asserting their cultural and even moral inferiority. It assigns to the other the perpetual status of dependent alien, deprived of the social resources needed to make a contribution to the geo-political protocol of up-keeping and managing the global household. The superiority complex and sense of entitlement exhibited by the West manifests a familiar colonizing attitude that reduces the majority world into an outlet for natural resources and a market for the overprized cultural, ideological, and material products of the West (often destructive to indigenous cultures and economies), for which someone else has to pay the price. Unfortunately, this attitude is often assumed and displayed also by the Western Church, including Western Pentecostalism which is not immune to exhibiting paternalistic tendencies towards Pentecostal movements in the global South.[73] However, the same demeaning attitude is also manifested by the assertion of Pentecostalism's spiritual superiority in the face of other Christian traditions, through postures of aggressive condemnation towards other religions, and by self-righteous justification of unrestrained exploitation of creation.

While reflecting on the cities of refuge, Levinas makes the important observation that Western society – free and civilized – enjoys riches and privileges, often at the expense of the rest of the world, causing the suffering and depravation of others (e.g. through neo-colonial exploitation or through unrestrained consumption of

---

[72] For more on the disempowerment of hospitality practiced from the position of cultural superiority see Pohl, *Making Room*, pp. 119-21.

[73] For more on this subject see Samuel Martinez, 'Pentecostalism and Postcolonialism: Toward a Planetary Spiritual Network', paper presented at the 41st Annual Meeting of the Society for Pentecostal Studies, Regent University, Virginia Beach, Virginia, February 29-March 3, 2012.

'cheap' goods produced in sweat shops within the developing world). With ignorant innocence we participate in manslaughter and act surprised when the anger of the world rages against us. In light of this volatile reality of our societal conscience, Levinas questions, 'does not all this make our cities cities of refuge or cities of exiles?'[74] Perhaps this is why the arrival of the stranger in our midst makes us more anxious than ever – we are not sure if they are not 'the avenger of blood'. Yet, in the words of Immanuel Kant, the fact that the earth is a globe means that we cannot be 'infinitely scattered, and must at the end reconcile ourselves to existence side by side'[75] with the other.

There is no question that if it is to contribute towards the transformation of the global village into a home for all of its dwellers, Western Pentecostalism has to recapture its own heritage of prophetic marginality and vulnerability in the face of the other, and commit to cultivating the spiritual discipline of solidarity with the oppressed, the exploited, and the marginalized over against its drive towards social acceptance and affluence. This is a commitment to being a sanctuary and an access to life for the other. To paraphrase the words of St. Irenaeus, ultimately, 'the glory of God is every creature fully alive'.[76] A Pentecostal commitment to upholding the glory of God (in the face of the ever pressing temptation of magnifying one's own significance and right to dismiss the other) will have to take seriously the work of the Spirit on the margins and at the boundaries of difference. Such a commitment will surrender the Pentecostal communal life to extending the hospitality of God to the other in ecumenical, ecological, and economic acts of home-building for all of God's creatures. This is home-building as giving access to life more abundant in the embrace of the Christoformed

---

[74] Levinas, *Beyond the Verse*, p. 40.

[75] Immanuel Kant, *Perpetual Peace: A Philosophical Essay* (trans. M. Campbell; New York & London: Grand Publishing, 1972), p. 138.

[76] This is a paraphrase of St. Irenaeous' statement, 'the glory of God is man fully alive'. The text continues: ' … moreover man's life is the vision of God: if God's revelation through creation has already obtained life for all the beings that dwell on earth, how much more will the Word's manifestation of the Father obtain life for those who see God' (*Adversus Haereses*, IV, 20, 7). The paraphrase captures the spirit of the text and was made famous by Sallie McFague's writings, especially, *Life Abundant: Rethinking Theology an Economy for a Planet in Peril* (Minneapolis, MN: Augsburg Fortress, 2001), p. 3.

human community where the Spirit remains the One and only host and giver of cosmic hospitality.

3

PENTECOST'S COMMUNAL ECONOMICS AND THE HOUSEHOLD OF GOD

Introduction

Three fundamental terms, packed with socio-political significance and tension, have their etymological origin in the Greek word *oikos* translated 'house' or 'household'. These are *ecology*, *economics*, and *ecumenism*.[1] Therefore, applying our linguistic imagination, we can think about ecology as 'words or discourse about the household', of economics as the 'management of the household and its resources', and of ecumenicity as 'the togetherness and interconnectivity within the household'. In our current planetary condition of economic and socio-political globalization we experience stronger than ever the functional connectivity between these three dimensions of human existence. We realize that our personal and societal well-being is intricately connected to the well-being of the globe and that we share each-others' dreams and nightmares in ways that once upon a time were merely a futuristic speculation. The process of globalization has challenged us with the realization that we are all members

---

[1] Exploring the connection between theology and economics, various scholars have reflected on the etymology of these terms. Noteworthy is Sallie McFague's idea of understanding ecology as 'words about home', being fundamental in developing ecological literacy and ecumenicity (Sallie McFague. *A New Climate for Theology: God, the World and Global Warming* [Minneapolis, MN: Fortress Press, 2008], p. 48).

of the same planetary household and share the responsibility for its welfare.

M. Douglas Meeks defines *oikos* as 'access to livelihood'.[2] For home

> is where everyone knows your name. Home is where you can always count on being comforted, forgiven, loved, and cared for. Home is where there is always a place for you at the table. And, finally, home is where you can count on sharing what is on the table.[3]

If we apply this poetic definition of home to planet Earth as the *oikos* of contemporary global society, we may conclude that almost two-thirds of the planet's population is homeless, for they live in poverty – in sub-human conditions with scarce access to livelihood.[4] As Daniel G. Groody remarks, when looked at from 'below', 'it becomes all the more evident that economic development in the global village has not always led to greater human development. Most of the world lacks the basic necessities for dignified human life'.[5] Economic justice has become the central question of the *oikonomia* of the global village, and receiving justice is receiving 'access to home'.[6] The inadequacies of economic development are further highlighted by the growing awareness of the interdependence between ecological, economic, and social sustainability. Therefore, concerns for economic justice have become closely linked with the demand for ecological justice as authors like Sallie McFague have identified nature as the 'new poor' in the North Atlantic economies and called for its emancipation and inclusion in the planetary household.[7]

---

[2] M. Douglas Meeks, *God the Economist: The Doctrine of God and Political Economy* (Minneapolis, MN: Fortress Press, 1989), p. 33.

[3] Meeks, *God the Economist*, p. 36.

[4] For statistics on poverty in the global village see Daniel G. Groody, 'Globalizing Solidarity: Christian Anthropology and the Challenge of Human Liberation', *Theological Studies* 69 (2008), pp. 250-68.

[5] Groody, 'Globalizing Solidarity', p. 258.

[6] Meeks, *God the Economist*, p. 36.

[7] Sallie McFague, 'An Ecological Christology: Does Christianity Have It?', in Dieter T. Hessel and Rosemary Redford Reuther (eds.) *Christianity and Ecology: Seeking the Well-Being of Earth and Humans* (Cambridge, MA: Harvard University Press, 2000), p. 30. See also McFague's work, *Life Abundant: Rethinking Theology*

A significant portion of modern economic history has been dominated by the so-called neo-classical economic model that clearly neglects the connection between economy and ecology, and reduces all other social relationships to economic functions of exchange and consumption navigated by self-interest. The father of neo-classical economics, Adam Smith, insisted that common good is an eventual outcome of the personal pursuit of wealth and economic self-interest. Smith asserted the guidance of society through 'the invisible hand' of divine providence in accomplishing the betterment of all while indulging individual interests and desires.[8] Other thinkers of the time agreed with Smith that personal greed functions as a virtue in this model of market economy since its final end leads to a richer society as a whole.[9]

This is the model that has produced contemporary 'market society' where market logic has permeated all dimensions of human existence and transformed them into realms of stock-exchange in satisfying personal needs and desires. The claim of market society is that everything can potentially be commodified and sold at the market, and that since the market is neutral, impersonal, and automatic it can function 'without systems of justice based on natural law'.[10] As Meeks points out, 'the great fascination of the market is the assumption that we have finally found a way to organize mass human behavior without dominion, authority and coercion'.[11] However, the all comprehensive 'objectivity' of the market is blind to the creation of non-marketable populace which is alienated from the cycle of production and consumption, by virtue of lacking market value. The weak, the young, the elderly and the handicapped are

---

and Economy for A Planet in Peril (Minneapolis, MN: Fortress Press, 2001), pp. 33-37.

[8] Adam Smith, *The Theory of Moral Sentiments* (New York: Augustus M. Kelley Publishers, 1966), p. 304. In this particular work Smith advocates a connection between human greed and divine providence in God's 'care of the universal happiness of all rational and sensible beings' (p. 210). For further reading on Smith's ideas about the function of self-interest see his work *An Inquiry into the Nature and Causes of the Wealth of Nations* (London: William Benton Publisher, 1955).

[9] Munyaradzi Felix Murove, 'Perceptions of Greed in Western Economic and Religious Traditions: An African Communitarian Response', *Black Theology* 5.2 (2007), pp. 220-43.

[10] Meeks, *God the Economist*, p. 38.

[11] Meeks, *God the Economist*, p. 38.

among this 'surplus'[12] humanity excluded from the bliss of market society.

The neo-classical model of economics is based on tracing the movement of exchange and trade of labor, goods, services, and other forms of capital between household units and companies. Within it, the household is merely a participating component that makes possible the continual free-market cycle of supply, production, exchange, and consumption. The survival of the household depends on the degree of its convertibility within the relationships mandated by market logic. Therefore, the household as a whole and its individual members are commodified and ascribed an exchange value which converts their intellectual, biological, and creative abilities into market commodities. This is a de-personified value, determined by supply and demand. This economic model manages humanity as one among the essential natural resources that facilitate the continuity of economic production and serves as an integral factor in determining the scope and character of production. However, the neo-classical economic model does not properly account for the input and output of energy and matter, thus creating the illusion of an economic process that functions as a *perpetuum mobile* – a perfect closed self-perpetuating system (engine) of production and consumption that exists irrespectively of the surrounding environment. Further, by ignoring the environment, the neo-classical model does not account for nature's participation in the economic process (e.g. as the source of energy and natural resources) and does not acknowledge the environmental effects of production (e.g. material pollution and energy waste). It also does not take under consideration the free contribution of Creation in the process of production and consumption (e.g. bee-pollination, water cycle and filtration, ozone layer protection, etc.).

In contrast to the neo-classical model, ecological economics highlights the inter-connectivity and interdependence between society, the environment, and the economic process. It brings to the surface the issues of ecology as integral to the wellbeing of humanity and the sustainability of economics. The recovered sense of in-

---

[12] In his work M.D. Meeks develops the concept of 'surplus people' who do not fit in the logic and cycles of market economy. See 'The Church and the Poor in Supply-Side Economics', *Cities* 1 (Fall 1983), pp. 6-9.

terdependence between ecology and economics makes this model more organic and communal. The flourishing of the separate individual becomes inexplicably connected to the flourishing of the whole (in all of its anthropic and non-anthropic components).[13] While the neo-classical model reflects the market logic and its priority of self-interest resulting in competition for resources, ecological economics is 'a human enterprise that seeks to maximize the optimal functioning of the planet's gifts and services for all users'.[14]

In further contrast to the neo-classical model, ecological economics views the economic and social spheres not as independent realms, but as co-dependent and positioned within the vaster environmental sphere. While reflecting the complexity and interdependence of social, environmental, and economic existence, and emphasizing human moral responsibility for the environment, ecological economics still treat the household unit as just an element within the economic process of production, consumption and sustainability.

Yet Christianity offers a different vision of household – the vision of the world's ultimate transfiguration into the house of God, into a sanctuary for all of His creatures. The incarnation of this vision is the charismatic creative work of the Holy Spirit, who transforms human beings and communities into Christ-likeness. The Spirit guides humanity towards its eschatological destiny – the Cosmic Christ – the redemptive *telos* of creation who is the Truth that sets us free and makes us whole as human beings, as communities and as a world.

Contrary to the traditional capitalist priority of economic self-interest,[15] the Christian vision of household insists on the practice of politics and economics as an external materialization of inner spiritual life and therefore, as 'the practice of morality'.[16] It upholds

---

[13] McFague. *A New Climate for Theology*, p. 88.

[14] McFague. *A New Climate for Theology*, p. 89.

[15] For a more detailed political and economic exposition on the wealth accumulating and consumption reflex of capitalism, see Alex Callinicos, *An Anti-Capitalist Manifesto* (Cambridge: Polity Press, 2003), pp. 35-39.

[16] Vaclav Havel, 'Politics, Morality and Civility', in Don E. Eberly (ed.), *The Essential Civil Society Reader: Classic Essays in the American Civil Society Debate* (Lanham, MD: Rowman & Littlefield, 2000) p. 397.

the necessity of covenantal civil society[17] insisting on taking responsibility for the wellbeing of the other and cultivating the civic virtue of fasting from oneself on behalf of the fellow human and the rest of creation. In this spiritual discipline one is committed to sharing possessions with one's neighbor and redistributing wealth according to human needs rather than political and economic benefits. The development of this type of civic consciousness requires humanity's transfiguration into the likeness of God.

The Pentecost communal economic model, as articulated by Luke in the Acts of the Apostles, exemplifies precisely this transfiguring spirituality within the Spirit-filled *koinonia* of believers. The Spirit transforms them into Christ-likeness, making them partakers of the divine nature and translating them into the life of the Trinity so that in turn they can become an incarnation of the divine communal life on earth. The community of faith becomes 'the household of God' so that through the agency of the Holy Spirit it may participate in God's work of transforming the entire world 'into a household in which all of God's creatures will find access to life.'[18]

The present chapter is inspired by the struggles of Eastern Europe in its difficult transition from planned to deregulated economy after the fall of communism, as well as by its disillusionment with the consumerist inversion of communal life within the new economic realities in this part of the world. In light of that, the chapter offers a brief overview of the rise of global neo-liberal capitalism and its advent in Eastern Europe. It further contrasts the ideological foundations of Western economic individualism and Eastern communitarianism and explores the theological foundations of Pentecost's model of communal economics and its underlying spirituality that follows the pattern of God's generous redemptive self-sharing with humanity and the rest of creation. Finally, the text highlights the function of the Eucharist in the community of faith

---

[17] Jonathan Sacks, *The Politics of Hope* (London: Vintage, 2000). The author describes the so-called 'third-sector institutions', those sustaining the civil society, in the conditions of late capitalism. He calls the relationships they form covenantal (vs. contractual) and sees them as foundational for just society.

Jean Bethke Elshtain also highlights the need for a 'new social covenant' in 'Democracy on Trial', in *The Essential Civil Society Reader*, pp. 101-22, esp. pp. 117-20.

[18] Meeks, *God the Economist*, p. 45.

as pedagogy of disciplining desires and teaching reverent consumption.

Between Individualism and Communitarianism[19]

The Rise of Global Neo-liberal Capitalism and Its Advent in Eastern Europe

The terms 'neo-liberal' and 'neo-classical' economics are often used interchangeably in contemporary economic jargon. Historically, they have emerged as identifiers of the contextualization of Adam Smith's classical economic theory within the conditions of the nineteenth and twentieth centuries. Therefore, there is nothing truly 'neo' in economic neo-liberalism. By the end of the nineteenth century Smith's assertion of 'the invisible hand' had been stripped of metaphysical implications and had become the impersonal 'hand of the markets' capable of 'mobilizing even the basest of human instincts such as gluttony, greed, and the desire for wealth and power for the benefit of all'.[20]

The origins of the twentieth-century reiteration of Smith's economic dogmatics could be traced to 1938 when a group of intellectuals met in Paris to discuss the rising threat of German National Socialism under Hitler and of collectivist economic planning (e.g. the British Keynesian and American New Deal policies). This meeting (organized by Louis Rougier) coined the term 'neo-liberalism' as an update of nineteenth-century liberalism 'by introducing the idea that governments play an important role as guardians of "free markets" by securing the rule of law'.[21]

During the 1980s neo-liberalism experienced a new boost as Thatcherism and Reaganomics introduced policies that represented

---

[19] The content of this section within the present chapter originated in my work 'Pentecost and Prosperity in Eastern Europe: Between Sharing of Possessions and Accumulating of Personal Wealth', in Katherine Attanasi and Amos Yong (eds.), *Pentecostalism and Prosperity: The Socio-Economics of the Global Charismatic Movements* (New York: Palgrave Macmillan, 2012), pp. 189-212.

[20] David Harvey, *A Brief History of Neoliberalism* (New York: Oxford University Press, 2005), p. 20.

[21] Kean Birch and Vlad Mykhnenko, 'Introduction: A World Turned Right Way Up', in Kean Birch and Vlad Mykhnenko (eds.), *The Rise and Fall of Neoliberalism: The Collapse of an Economic Order* (New York: Zed Books, 2010), p. 3.

'"rolling-back" of regulations, state ownership and welfare services'.[22] In 1989, the year in which the world witnessed in disbelief the fall of the Berlin Wall and the lifting of the Iron Curtain that had partitioned the East from the West for almost half a century, John Williamson outlined ten policy reforms towards market deregulation that consequently became known as the Washington Consensus. They served in the next decades as the universal programmatic of the global advancement of neo-liberal capitalism and included the following elements:

> … an imposition of a tight fiscal discipline (… no public budget deficit allowed); an end to subsidies and re-direction of public expenditure on basic health, education and infrastructure; tax cuts; financial liberalization; free-floating exchange rates; trade liberalization with an unified low tariff; openness to foreign direct investment; privatization; deregulation; and secure private property rights.[23]

These were precisely the measures demanded by the World Bank and the International Monetary Fund as the conditions for their financial intervention in Eastern Europe. The Washington Consensus promised renewed growth and prosperity to the uttermost parts of the globe by 'the unleashing of markets – the basic enabling reform from which all the potential benefits of transition follow'.[24] However, instead of the anticipated results, it created within the region an unprecedented depression.[25]

The ideology of transition from planned to market economy was also identified as the only guarantor of the democratic political process. The proponents of neo-liberalism (e.g. Milton Friedman) insisted that 'because profit-making is the essence of democracy, any government that pursues anti-market policies is being anti-democratic'.[26] Of course, no government in the post-communist

---

22 Birch and Mykhnenko, 'Introduction', p. 7.

23 Birch and Mykhnenko, 'Introduction', p. 9.

24 World Bank, *World Development Report 1996: From Plan to Market* (Oxford: Oxford University Press, 1996): at (http://wdronline.worldbank.org//worldbank/a/c.html/world_development_report_1996/part_challenge_transition).

25 Birch and Mykhnenko, 'Introduction', p. 11.

26 Robert W. McChesney, 'Introduction', in Noam Chromsky, *Profit over People: Neoliberalism and Global Order* (New York: Steven Stories Press, 1999), p. 9.

Eastern European countries wanted to be labeled as anti-democratic. Therefore, regardless of the unstable political environment and the often-changing successions of 'right' and 'left' governments, all political competitors were eager to meet the demands of the West for the liberalization of the markets. Robert W. McChesney has argued that the assertion of the 'sacredness' of the market actually had a demoralizing and deconstructive effect on the democratic process because it eventually depoliticized the citizens. 'If electoral democracy affects little of social life, it is irrational to devote much attention to it'.[27] Such logic would naturally lead to political apathy. This was precisely the case in the Eastern European countries. In the first decade of transition there was a gradual depolitization of the population as it realized that new elections would not produce significant change in socio-economic life. McChesney further insists that

> Neoliberal democracy with its notion of the market *über alles*, takes dead aim at this sector. Instead of citizens, it produces consumers. Instead of communities, it produces shopping malls. The net result is an atomized society of disengaged individuals who feel demoralized and socially powerless.[28]

The transition to neo-liberal capitalism in Eastern Europe has been a difficult and turbulent process of adaptation to new ideological, economic, and political realities often perceived as necessary evils for one's survival in the contemporary global village.

Reflecting on the economic developments under the transition from communism to capitalism in Central Europe, Andrew Stroehlein does not hide his disappointment with the effects of market liberalization as he asserts that in Czech society, 'money-making defeated morals hands down in the 1990s, as those with connections scrambled to get the rich pickings offered by privatization'.[29] The era was well-summarized by Vaclav Klaus' infamous statement: 'There is no dirty money'.[30]

---

[27] McChesney, 'Introduction', p. 10.

[28] McChesney, 'Introduction', p. 11.

[29] Andrew Stroehlein, 'Three Vaclavs', *Central Europe Review* 1.10 (30 August, 1999), p. 3.

[30] Stroehlein, 'Three Vaclavs', p. 3.

Under the paradoxical transformation of capitalist political economy, the former communist elite became the new capitalist oligarchy due to their exclusive access to the financial resources needed for the privatization of the formerly state-owned means of production. Exploiting the vulnerability and confusion of the populous in its disillusionment with the new capitalist reality, the former communist elite renamed its political party, re-vocabularized its pre-election platform, and (by the mid 1990s) succeeded to emerge once again as the leading political power in most of the Eastern-European countries. The former president of the Czech Republic, Vaclav Havel, made the following statement about this cynical twist in the political and economic life of the post-communist societies:

> Demagogy is rife, and even something as important as the natural longing of a people for autonomy is exploited in power plays, as rivals compete in lying to the public. Many members of the party elite, the so-called *nomenklatura* who, until very recently, were faking concern about social justice and the working class, have cast aside their masks and, almost overnight, openly became speculators and thieves. Many a once-feared Communist is now an unscrupulous capitalist, shameless and unequivocally laughing in the face of the same workers whose interests he once allegedly defended.[31]

The shift from communism to deregulated markets introduced new disturbing and depressing socio-economic realities. The 'shock therapy' approach 'strongly advocated by the U.S. Treasury and the IMF'[32] found the population unprepared to cope with the transition. Amidst staggering unemployment and escalating inflation rates, the Eastern European countries experienced the systemic mass-impoverishment and economic displacement of entire demographic groups (the elderly, the single parents and their children, the

---

[31] Vaclav Havel, 'Politics, Morality and Civility', in Don E. Eberly (ed.), *The Essential Civil Society Reader: Classic Essays in the American Civil Society Debate* (Lanham, MD: Rowman & Littlefield Publishers, 2000), p. 392.

[32] Joseph E. Stiglitz, *Globalization and its Discontents* (New York & London: W.W. Norton & Company, 2002), p. 141. Stiglitz, winner of the Nobel Prize in economics and former chief economist and senior vice president of the World Bank, offers a comprehensive analysis of the failure of the 'shock therapy' approach in Russia (pp. 133-65).

Roma ethnic minorities). As the former vice president of the World Bank, Josef E Stiglitz asserts,

> Globalization and the introduction of market economy has not produced the promised results in Russia and most of the other economies making the transition from communism to the market ... in many respects, for most of the people, the market economy proved even worse than their Communist leaders had predicted.[33]

Eastern Europeans further witnessed the appearance of various negative social sub-products of the capitalist economic arrangement, namely: feminization of poverty[34] and commodification of femininity,[35] child and adult homelessness, juvenile alcoholism and drug abuse, escalating crime and violence.[36] Further, the lack of stable institutions and corresponding legislation regulating economics in the new post-communist conditions contributed to the flourishing of criminal activity in the economic sector and in society at large.[37]

---

[33] Stiglitz, *Globalization and its Discontents*, p. 6.

[34] Swanee Hunt, 'Raising Their Voices: Women in the New Democracies', *The Ambassadors Review* (Fall 1997) (the full text is at http://www.ksg.harvard.edu wappp/happen/raising_voices.pdf).

[35] Regarding the gender dimension of exploitation and global feminization of labor see also: Beruch Berberoglu, *Globalization of Capital and the Nation-State: Imperialism, Class Struggle, and the State in the Age of Global Capitalism* (Lanham, MD: Rowman & Littlefield, 2003), p. 4; Jill Steans, 'Globalization and Gender Inequality', in David Held and Anthony McGrew (eds.), *The Global Transformations Reader*, 2nd ed. (Oxford: Polity, 2003), pp. 455-63. See also Tiffany G. Petros, 'Mop, Shop and Shut up: Feminism in the Czech Republic', *Central Europe Review* 2.43 (11 December 2000): at (http://www.ce-review.org/00/43/petros43); and Lucy Ward, 'After the Wall', *Guardian* (Thursday, 23 September, 1999): at (http://www.guar dian.co.uk/print/0,3858,3904787-103691,00.html).

[36] Concerning the negative effect the transition to capitalism and Western liberal democracy has had on Eastern Europe, see also Berberoglu, *Globalization of Capital and the Nation-State*, p. 10. The author sees the exploitation of raw materials in Eastern Europe by Western capitalism as a form of neo-colonialism.

[37] Accumulation of personal wealth became often associated with illegal activities: from acts of corruption and tax evasion to misappropriation of governmental funds and organized crime. The early stories of personal economic success often had a dark and hidden side. While the illegal origin of the wealth of many new capitalists was a matter of common knowledge, they were rarely summoned to responsibility in the public domain. The population felt traumatized by the criminalization of economic life. In addition to the lack of stable institutions and corresponding legislation regulating economics in the new post-communist con-

Civil Society was virtually non-existent in the communist past of the Eastern European countries. Holmes suggests that

> … most cases in which the masses played a significant role in overthrowing communist power should be seen as examples of protest politics, not the power of civil society.[38]

The process of developing and empowering civil society in the former Eastern Block has been a complex and difficult task. The advent of neo-liberalism with its emphasis on individualism over against the pursuit of the common societal good further complicated the process of nurturing and developing civil initiative and responsibility.

The attitude of the radical market-oriented rhetoric broadcasted within the newly-freed-world of the East could be summarized by Margaret Thatcher's famous phrase, 'There is no such thing as the social. There are only individuals and families.'[39] This view was quickly adopted by prominent pragmatic political voices who displayed an open hostility towards the concept and function of civil society. The current president of the Czech Republic, Vaclav Klaus, in contrast to his famous predecessor, Vaclav Havel,[40] has openly rejected civil society and called it 'aberrant'. 'He has consistently refused to accept the idea that non-profit organizations could help

---

ditions, racketeering was often quoted as one of the causes for bankruptcy of small businesses and as a reason contributing to the difficulties in the development of middle class in the post-communist countries. The story of Leonid Chernovet'skyi described by Catherine Wanner in her book *Communities of the Converted: Ukrainians and Global Evangelism* (Ithaca and London: Cornell University Press, 2007), pp. 236-39, illustrates the assertion that most of the new capitalists with a significant personal wealth were associated with the old communist regime as well as with some illegal activities.

[38] Leslie Holmes, *Rotten States? Corruption, Post-Communism and Neoliberalism* (Durham and London: Duke University Press, 2006), p. 186. There are obvious exceptions to this statement. For example, one should consider the impact of *Solidarnost* in Poland upon the socio-economic and political transformation of society before the fall of communism. Another particularity of the Polish case is the role of the Catholic Church for the formation and maintaining the existence of civil society under communism.

[39] Interview with Margaret Thatcher in the weekly periodical *Woman's Own*, London (July 1987). See also Stroehlein, 'Three Vaclavs, p. 2.

[40] Regarding the difference between the views of Vaclav Havel and Vaclav Klaus see 'Rival Visions: Vaclav Havel and Vaclav Klaus' with commentary by Petr Rithart, *Journal of Democracy* 7.1 (1996), pp. 12-23.

the country as much as profit-making ones'.[41] Recognizing the influence that non-governmental organizations are gaining in the Czech Republic and reflecting on their impact on the political process, Klaus took an offensive stand against the role of NGOs arguing that they claim political power they never received in elections, and stated that they represent a 'threat to democracy'.[42] This obvious lack of understanding of the role of civil society is symptomatic of the absence of legacy of multilateral dialogue and collaboration in the pursuit of the common good within the frame of a civil covenant.

As Eastern Europe struggled to make the transition from planned to deregulated market economy, the countries within the region wrestled ideologically and ethically with the pressure of market-driven life and its demands both for conversion from communitarianism to individualism and from emphasis on production to preoccupation with consumption.[43] Despite the eventual accommodation of capitalism's demands, much of the population in the region shares a sense of disillusionment with the democratic process and the capitalist market economy, which (on the background of surging nationalism) are perceived as Western impositions that have jeopardized any possibility of developing indigenous models of political and economic life.

Much of the Eastern European negative attitude towards Western neo-liberalism clearly has its roots within the secular and reli-

---

[41] Stroehlein, 'Three Vaclavs', p. 3. Carol Stalik Left, *The Czech and Slovak Republics: Nation Versus State* (Oxford: Westview Press, 1997), p. 157.

[42] Jan Richter, 'Vaclav Klaus: The Experienced and Predictable', Radio Prague, Special Edition (February 7, 2008), p. 2, (http://www.radio.cz/en/section/election-special/vaclav-klaus-the-exp...).

[43] Amidst this context of transition towards deregulated markets, the prosperity gospel was introduced in Eastern Europe as the Western religious counterpart of neo-liberalism. The prosperity gospel offered a coping mechanism amidst the turmoil of this overwhelming societal change. It offered a scriptural justification and moral foundation for the embrace of capitalist market economy, and it promoted capitalist values by encouraging private enterprise, consumer choice, personal responsibility, and entrepreneurial initiative. By placing a Christian sanction upon the individual pursuit of wealth and consumerist indulgence, the prosperity message accommodated the conditions of the market crowning it with a 'halo' and connecting it to the providential justice of God. For more on the effects of the prosperity gospel in Eastern Europe, see Augustine, 'Pentecost and Prosperity in Eastern Europe', pp. 189-212.

gious communitarianism that has shaped this part of the world. In light of the apparent contrast between the ideological backgrounds of the East and the West, the following two sub-sections in this chapter offer a brief examination of the religious and economic foundations of Western neo-liberal capitalism and Eastern European communitarianism.

Ideological Foundations of Western Neo-Liberal Capitalism: Adam Smith and the Calvinist Accommodation of the Spirit of Capitalism

The development of Adam Smith's political economy is situated within the context of the eighteenth-century Calvinist 'Protestant ethic'. Karl Polanyi points out that Smith, while serving as a professor of moral philosophy in the University of Glasgow, 'publicly ascribed his assent to the Calvinist Confession of Faith before the Presbytery' of the city.[44] While a superficial reading of his work in economics may give an impression of a secular rationale in support of his analyses and corresponding conclusions, many researchers have suggested that we view Smith as a 'life-long moral philosopher, who never casts aside his earlier concerns about human morality in his later pursuit of economic truths'.[45] Such an understanding of Smith necessitates keeping in dialectical tension his two main works, namely, *The Theory of Moral Sentiments* and *An Inquiry into the Nature and Causes of the Wealth of Nations*, and it assumes that the second text is somehow informed and shaped by the first. If this is true, 'then Smith can be seen as promoting an economic model that is based on socially sanctioned ethical norms supported by appropriate and just social institutions'.[46] Some authors go as far as to suggest that Smith is in fact a moral theologian and that his elaboration on the 'invisible hand' is 'his particular contribution to eighteenth–century theodicy'.[47] For example, Kathryn Blanchard insists

[44] Karl Polanyi, *The Great Transformation: The Political and Economic Origins of Our Times* (New York: Farrar, Straus & Giroux, 1975), p. 333.

[45] Kathryn D. Blanchard, *The Protestant Ethic or the Spirit of Capitalism: Christians, Freedom, and Free Markets* (Eugene, OR: Cascade Books, 2010), p. 57.

[46] Blanchard, *The Protestant Ethic or the Spirit of Capitalism*, p. 57.

[47] Lisa Hill, 'The Hidden Theology of Adam Smith', *European Journal of the History of Economic Thought* 8.1 (2001), p. 22. Hill articulates the various interpretations of function of 'the invisible hand' in Smith's work, e.g. lexical and metaphorical, critical and ironic, evolutionary Darwinian, theological assertion of di-

that Smith's anthropology, as articulated in his *Theory of Moral Sentiments*, 'presents not self-interest but intellectual approbation and natural sympathy as the primary characteristics of the human being'. She summarizes Smith's conclusion: 'At the bottom it is sympathy people want, not material pleasures'.[48]

Smith's moral philosophy renders visible the tension between the individualistic impulse of the separate human being and the unavoidable social dimensions of human existence. Smith views the urge for social acceptance and inter-human connectivity as having been pre-wired in human conscience and manifested in a shared commitment to justice for one's own sake. Therefore, one's personal happiness and wellbeing motivates one toward justice. Smith asserts that

> Every man is, no doubt, by nature, first and principally recommended to his own care; and as he is fitter to take care of himself, than of any other person, it is fit and right that it should be so ... Though it may be true, therefore, that every individual, in his own breast, naturally prefers himself to all mankind, yet he dares not look mankind in the face, and avow that he acts according to this principle.[49]

Smith continues by stating that in the 'race for wealth' a person may 'outstrip all his competitors', but if in the process he 'injures' any of them, society will sympathize with the victim and direct its 'hatred and indignation' towards the one who has caused their misfortune.[50] The threat of social isolation, public shame, and consternation motivate moral restraint in relation to one's passions and desires. Thus, ultimately love of self (not love of neighbor) helps moral agents navigate between sociality and natural hedonistic tendencies.

Wealth, however, also secures social acceptance based on fame and envious admiration.[51] Thus, Smith states his thesis that 'we

---

vine providence, etc.

48 Blanchard, *The Protestant Ethic or the Spirit of Capitalism*, 65.

49 Adam Smith, *The Theory of Moral Sentiments* (New York: Augustus M. Kelley Publishers, 1966), pp. 119-20.

50 Smith, *The Theory of Moral Sentiments*, p. 120.

51 As Smith states: 'The rich man glories in his riches, because he feels that they naturally draw upon him the attention of the world, and that mankind are

make parade of our riches, and conceal our poverty' because the world is predisposed to sympathize more with joy than with sorrow, and we long for its sympathy.[52] Reflecting upon Smith's emphasis on the human need and capacity for sympathy, Blanchard points out that Smith identifies 'humanity' not in terms of *homo economicus* but as *homo sympatheticus*.[53] Yet, Smith's thesis mediates an overwhelming sense of loneliness. As the separate individual faces the predicates of social acceptance and approval, he/she is caged by the internal struggle between self-indulgence and propriety, between self-love and the need for the sympathy of others. Perhaps, this nuance of Smith's anthropology can be viewed as an outcome of its broader context shaped by Calvinist soteriology, with its introverted preoccupation with personal salvation and outward competition in proving one's position among the elect.

In his famous (and continually debated)[54] reflection on the social and psychological effects of Calvin's doctrine of election, Max Weber points out that this doctrine resulted in 'a feeling of tremendous inner loneliness' and despair that demanded an intervention.[55] This intervention according to Weber was 'work' – diligent persistence in one's calling (or vocation) in the world as an act of worship to God and proof of one's belonging among the elect.[56] Weber argued that this fusion of the doctrines of predestination and vocation birthed a form of asceticism expressed in hard work and abstinence from worldly pleasures that produced a new form of economic life associated with the rise of capitalism. However, it also created the ideological foundations for the shift from communitarianism to individualism within the spiritual, political, and economic dimensions

disposed to go along with him in all those agreeable emotions with which the advantages of his situation so readily inspire him. At the thought of this his heart seems to swell and dilate itself within him, and he is fonder of his wealth, upon this account, than for all the other advantages it procures him. The poor man, on the contrary is ashamed of his poverty' (Smith, *The Theory of Moral Sentiments*, p. 71).

[52] Smith, *The Theory of Moral Sentiments*, p. 70.

[53] Blanchard, *The Protestant Ethic or the Spirit of Capitalism*, p. 67.

[54] For a sample of critical engagement with Weber's work, see Robert W. Green (ed.), *Protestantism and Capitalism: The Weber Thesis and Its Critics* (Boston: D. C. Heath and Company, 1959).

[55] Max Weber, *The Protestant Ethic and the 'Spirit' of Capitalism* (New York: The Penguin Group, 2002), p. 73.

[56] Weber, *The Protestant Ethic and the 'Spirit' of Capitalism*, p. 69, pp. 74-78.

of human existence, and deconstructed the religious and secular motivation for search of social redemption.

In contrast to Roman Catholicism's traditional suspicion and disapproval of accumulation of personal wealth, Calvinism offered a justification of the bourgeois economic vision and solidified the ideological foundations of the emerging middle class. While advocating moderation in relation to earthly pleasures, Calvin asserted that 'gold and riches' are 'good creations of God, permitted, indeed appointed, for men's use by God's providence' and insisted that all wealth in society is distributed according to God's justice.[57] The last assertion, however, has led scholars to believe that Calvin's primary concern was maintaining social stability and securing the existing status quo between the bourgeoisie and the poor. Therefore, his theological ethic promotes not economic equality but the elimination of social discontent which could potentially result in a demand for redistribution of wealth through civic, revolutionary, or (motivated by economic despair) criminal activity. However, most scholars would agree that Calvin's 'work ethic' was motivated by 'creating justice, sobriety, moderation and true worship of God among believers'.[58] Personal accumulation of wealth, therefore, was an unintended side-effect of the hard work and spending discipline of the Protestant population. As George Thomas has argued, it may be a mistake 'to speak of Calvin or his early followers as defenders of economic individualism'.[59] After all, he also insists on just prices and emphasizes a moral obligation toward good stewardship in the use of wealth.[60] Likewise, as Thomas Neil points out, if the later followers of Calvin had subscribed to his words against extortion, greed, exploitation, and high interest rates, 'Calvinism might have been a deterrent rather than a promoter of the capitalistic spirit'.[61]

Both Calvin's and Adam Smith's reflections on the economic life proceed from the particularity and limitations of their personal economic experience. They both belonged to the economically privi-

---

57 John Calvin, *Institutes of the Christian Religion* (trans. Ford Lewis Battles; ed. John T. McNeil; Philadelphia: Westminster, 1960), pp. III, XIX, 9.

58 Blanchard, *The Protestant Ethic or the Spirit of Capitalism*, p. 47.

59 George Thomas, *Christian Ethics and Moral Philosophy* (New York: Scribners, 1955), p. 309.

60 Blanchard, *The Protestant Ethic or the Spirit of Capitalism*, p. 45.

61 Thomas Neill, *Makers of the Modern Mind* (Milwaukee: Bruce, 1949), p. 43.

leged classes of their day. Calvin's theology did not adopt the perspective of the poor and economically marginalized. As Blanchard points out, Calvin 'seems to be writing for the rising bourgeoisie … who suddenly found themselves possessing a growing amount of worldly wealth and are in need of advice how best to manage it'.[62] In a similar manner, Smith's conclusions ignore the staggering misery of the poor in eighteenth-century England and develop the faulty assertion that 'the wages of the meanest laborer can supply' all of his/her existential need and further afford even various conveniences and occasional luxuries.[63] As Smith discusses the principles of the division of labor in the *Wealth of Nations*, he points to the relativity of wealth across different national and continental contexts, but fails to compare the economic conditions of the extremes present in his own country and the rest of Europe.[64] The division of labor, according to Smith, is motivated not by ingenuity, efficiency, and idealistic commitment to progress, but by individual self-interest, for

> … man has almost constant occasion for the help of his brethren, and it is in vain for him to expect it from their benevolence only. He will more likely prevail if he can interest their self-love in his favor, and show them that it is for their own advantage to do for him what he requires of them.[65]

The motive of self-interest permeates also Smith's discussion of the pros and cons of giving home market monopoly to domestic production versus imported goods. This is the context within which his argument introduces the legendary concept of the 'invisible hand' promoting the common good through the prioritization of one's personal benefit.[66] Smith insists: 'I have never known much good

---

62 Blanchard, *The Protestant Ethic or the Spirit of Capitalism*, p. 45.

63 Smith, *The Theory of Moral Sentiments*, p. 70.

64 Adam Smith, *An Inquiry into the Nature and Causes of the Wealth of Nations* (London: William Benton Publisher, 1955), p. 6.

65 Smith, *The Wealth of Nations*, p. 15.

66 The separate individual 'intends only his own gain'; however, the individual is ultimately led '… by an invisible hand to promote an end which was no part of his intention … By pursuing his own interest he frequently promotes that of the society more effectually than when he really intends to promote it' (Smith, *The Wealth of Nations*, p. 194).

done by those who affected to trade for the public good'.[67] Smith continues the passage with a statement against government regulation of the movement of private capital describing any intervention in the natural flow of the market process as unnecessary, dangerous, and presumptuous. Thus, he sums up the very essence of neoliberal economics.

Regardless of its various theological and secular interpretations, *The Wealth of Nations* clearly establishes Smith as the father of neoclassical economics and the forerunner of a deregulated global market. Thus, Smith is credited with supplying not only the foundations of the laissez-faire approach but also with giving it the moral justification needed for its flourishing in the West. Reflecting on the indebtedness of nineteen-century political economy to Smith, Eric Mount Jr. points out that the individualism fostered by its ideological effects 'remains a formidable force among us after two hundred years of our history ... In many ways it is our myth and our religion, our ethos and our ethic. It is manifestly, at least for now, our destiny.'[68]

Ideological Foundations of Eastern European Communitarianism

Eastern Europe is historically and geographically removed from the ideological context of the Reformation (and its preoccupation with personal salvation) and is predominantly[69] positioned within the Eastern Orthodox Tradition with its emphasis on cosmic redemption initiated by the proto-community of the social Trinity and carried forth by the Church. The community of faith that continues the divinely mandated ministry of reconciliation is called to consecrate the world through its life as an extension of Christ and, therefore, as an icon of the Triune God within the created order.

---

67 Smith, *The Wealth of Nations*, p. 194.

68 C. Eric Mount Jr., 'American Individualism Reconsidered', *Review of Religious Research* 22.4 (June 1981), p. 366.

69 An obvious exception in this regard will be the Central European post-communist countries (Poland, Slovakia, Czech Republic, and Hungary), which were historically and culturally associated with the West which places them within the influence spheres of Catholicism and Protestantism. However, the Eastern European countries are traditionally Eastern Orthodox and this is the religious affiliation of more than 90 percent of the population in this part of the world.

While the twentieth-century communist regimes in this part of the world appropriated Marx's secular dogmatics and numbered religion among the ideological enemies of the proletarian state, they still advocated communitarianism of shared possessions and prioritization of the common good over one's personal interest. Marxism represented a secularized version of the Pentecost communal economics of apostolic Christianity. Marx's motto, 'From everyone according to their abilities to everyone according to their needs' was directly inspired by the narrative of the Acts of the Apostles. Early Marxist critiques of institutionalized religion continually engaged the images of the post-Pentecost transformation of the community's economic life and insisted on the failure of the institutionalized ecclesia in fulfilling its own mission in the world as an instrument of political and economic justice. In fact, this failure is used as one of the moral justifications of the historical rise of communism. However, many Marxist thinkers have questioned the sustainability of the Pentecost economic model and have identified the sharing of products without sharing the means of production as the primary reason for its decline and eventual disappearance.[70] Therefore, Marxism outlines among the immediate objectives of the proletarian revolution the nationalization of the means of industrial production, followed by the de-privatization of the land and all natural resources.

Both the Christian and Marxist communitarian visions insist on the need for a 'new humanity' with 'new consciousness' that prioritizes the well-being of neighbor over personal interest. However, these visions identify different origins of this new saintly human being. In Christianity, he/she is God's new creation in Christ through the agency of the Holy Spirit who steps into history as an instrument of social transformation advancing the sociopolitical reality of the Kingdom as a movement of the Spirit from the innermost being to the uttermost parts of the world. In Marxism, conversely, the appearance of the new humanity is a product of a social evolution in which labor and ideological formation induce the birth of the new human consciousness that brings about the ultimate elimination of all classes and of the state itself into one global

[70] Rosa Luxemburg, 'Socialism and the Churches', *Marxist Classics*, (http://www.newyouth.com/archives/clssics/luxemburg/socialismandthechurches.html.

egalitarian society. In the first case, society is transfigured by the sovereign reign of God within humanity while moral responsibility for just social transformation resides with the believer and his/her community of faith within the world. This vision generates an extroverted movement of spiritual change that apprehends the world into its future one person at a time. In the second case, a violent proletarian revolution interrupts history and seizes its paths, insisting on its moral right to establish a dictatorship over the present based on its self-designation as the only class of the future. By eliminating all dissenting voices and systematically exterminating all independent socio-political imagination capable of envisioning alternative worlds, the communist vision of the proletarian state tries to establish the proper conditions needed to garden and grow the new human consciousness that will secure its uncontested ideological rule on earth. The first vision is that of God transfiguring the world into his likeness – the likeness of the social Trinity as diversity in unity. The second is that of humanity compressing the world into its own likeness until it is molded into a single, easily manageable homogeneity.

Orthodox Christianity views one's material existence (including one's personal possessions) as an outward extension of the person's inner life. Matter is understood as originating from the realm of the spirit – from the Creator God who reaches into the world through the synergy of his Word and Spirit bringing forth reality out of nothing. Marxism, conversely, views all spiritual (intellectual, ideological, artistic) life of humanity as proceeding from its material existence. Economics represents the fundamental base of the human experience and all other dimensions of individual and corporate human life are built upon this foundation as its ideological extension and reflection.

Traditionally, Eastern Orthodox theology has taken a critical stand towards both capitalism and Marxist socialism. Nicolas (Nikolai) Berdyaev, one of the most prominent Russian Orthodox thinkers of the early 1900s summarizes this dual critique in his reflections on the Marxist revolution. Berdyaev asserts that both capitalism and socialism are ultimately motivated by individualism, and their displays of concern for the common good cannot be separated from this prioritizing of self-interest.[71] Both capitalism and socialism have substituted the spiritual goals of life with material means; both economic models are therefore unable to sustain authentic human rights and freedom (since these represent high spiritual goals and have a spiritual origin).[72] Berdyaev points out that 'the historical material force is a part of the spiritual historical reality' and that 'the entire economic life of humanity has a spiritual base, a spiritual foundation'.[73] According to Berdyaev, the individualist inversion of social vision, as well as the secularization and fetishism of materialism and economism is 'a violation of the natural hierarchism of human society'.[74] Economic individualism substituted truth with Mammonism by presenting itself as superior in the pursuit of truth and attaining freedom from illusions. 'Economic Materialism', in turn, 'has formulated this in a most perfect way by declaring the entire spiritual life of the human as being an illusion and a fraud'.[75] In view of this, 'socialism is only a further development of the industrial capitalist system; it is the final celebration of its beginnings and a triumph of their universal spread'.[76] Berdyaev concludes that both 'Capitalism and Socialism are accompanied by decline and deflating of spiritual creativity, as a result of the recession of spirituality in human society'.[77] Therefore, any expectation of social transformation that facilitates authentic human freedom and justice would demand a 'revolution of the Spirit'.[78] Only the Spirit creates a brotherhood and sisterhood that are a realization of true freedom – as freedom in Christ. In the Christ-centered spiritual togetherness (*sobornost*)[79] there is no 'mechanical equality'. There is

---

[71] Nicolas Berdyaev, *The New Middle Ages*, in vol. 2 of *Collected Works* (Sofia: Zachari Stoyanov, 2003), pp. 526, 530-31.

[72] Nicolas Berdyaev, *Philosophy of Inequality* (Sofia: Prozoretz, 1923), pp. 110, 116.

[73] Nicolas Berdyaev, *The Meaning of History*, in vol. 2 of *Collected Works* (Sofia: Zachari Stoyanov, 2003), p. 313.

[74] Berdyaev, *The New Middle Ages*, p. 531.

[75] Berdyaev, *The New Middle Ages*, p. 531.

[76] Berdyaev, *The New Middle Ages*, p. 531.

[77] Berdyaev, *The New Middle Ages*, p. 532.

[78] Berdyaev, *The New Middle Ages*, p. 522.

[79] The theological concept of *sobornost* is fundamental for understanding the commitment to communitarian life within the Eastern Orthodox tradition. The *sobornost* of the faith community is the work of the Spirit who translates the communal life of the Trinity within the community of believers, making possible

also no contradiction and difference between 'a right and an obligation'.[80] The personal freedom in the Spirit's *sobornost* does not contradict the freedom of the other, for it is not based on competition for the limited resources of the material reality. It is based rather on the eternal and infinite reality of divine love and grace. In this divinely initiated and infused *sobornost*, the hospitality of God is incarnated in the community of Christ as a gift of the Spirit, a gift of freedom to the other to be and to become.

On the day of Pentecost the *sobornost* of the socio-economic reality of the Kingdom of God is birthed in the womb of the Church by the Spirit of God. The outcome is holy, for it is the doing of God Himself. As the Spirit tabernacles in the community of God, Christ's Body, the Church, becomes a temple, a Holy of Holies of His presence on earth. Nothing impure can survive in it, for in Him there is not a shadow of darkness (1 Jn 1.5). As the beauty of this brilliant light finds an expression in the sharing of possessions, humanity is freed for its destiny of Christ-likeness in sharing oneself with the other – a sacrament of self-giving and partaking in the other as partaking in God.

Pentecost's Communal Economics

Pentecost and the Self-sharing of the Creator and His Creation

If we look closely at the function of Creation within the economic process we will notice a different form of economic participation that does not follow market logic. Creation is not compensated for its contribution – therefore it does not participate in the economic exchange, but follows a model of sharing itself (and its resources) with humanity. It follows the model of the self-sharing and hospitality of its Creator.

The Word of God brought forth the non-anthropic Creation as a tangible materialization of its presence in the cosmos. This ontology reminds us of the spiritual origin of matter, but also points to the creation's function as a material dimension of God's love to-

---

sharing life with the other in all of its wholeness. This wholeness involves also the sharing of material existence (including personal possessions).

[80] Berdyaev, *Philosophy of Inequality*, p. 115.

wards humanity and the rest of His creatures in the divine creative self-giving and self-sharing with the other. The world therefore points back to the Word (Ps. 19.1-6) and, as Dimitru Staniloae asserts, becomes a witness and sign of the Word, bearing in itself the Word's divine presence and teleological intent.[81] Therefore, matter has a spiritual origin, content, and purpose which are inseparable from its design. The cosmos is filled with the Word's imprint which identifies not only the authorship, but also the ownership of God. As was already discussed in Chapter 2, God creates and gifts the world to humanity in an act of self-sharing so that humanity in turn may learn to share it with the other and the different. Therefore, the world is a gift with a pedagogical purpose forming humanity into the likeness of God. The world is a gift of unconditional divine hospitality manifested in God's self-limitation on behalf of the other. Therefore, attaining the likeness of the divine life within the human community demands one's personal 're-spacing' for the sake of the other within the covenantal bonds with God and neighbor.

In light of this, hospitality as obligation can be contrasted with hospitality as a gift from the Spirit (Rom. 12.13). Being the creation of the Holy Spirit, the faith community exhibits this self-sharing hospitality in the Body of Christ as an extension of God's welcoming the other expressed in bearing forth the fruit of the Spirit (Gal. 5.22-23). This fruit is produced in inter-sociality for the sake of the other and the different, as an act of Christ-like self-giving in love. This is a distinct type of production which implies a different political economy – one that builds its forms and relationships as an extension of the covenantal bonds needed for bearing forth this new social capital. Christ-like productivity brings forth a consciousness that prioritizes the needs of the other and meets them in hospitality of faith, hope, and love. This hospitality demands the re-spacing of the self and the redistribution of one's resources. It creates new conditions for the host in which the supplying of his or her personal needs becomes a function of supplying the needs of the other. Their own nurture becomes indispensable from 'doing the will of

---

[81] Dimitru Staniloae, *The Experience of God: Orthodox Dogmatic Theology*, vol. 2 *The World: Creation and Deification* (Brookline, MA: Holy Cross Orthodox Press, 2005), p. 21.

the Father' and accomplishing 'His work' as an extension of Christ on earth (Jn 4.34).

Ultimately, it is the hospitality of God that is offered and received by the other through the agency of the Spirit. This is the Creator's home-building, self-sharing hospitality which makes the cosmos a household for all – a home where all have a place at the table in the unconditionally loving embrace of the Trinity.

The event of Pentecost that marks the conception of Christ in the community of faith through the agency of the Spirit is also brought about through God's transformational self-giving. The salvific covenant has been initiated in the *kenosis* of the Son and sealed in the *kenosis* of the Spirit. The Pentecost theophany of the Spirit descending upon the believers confirms their identity as the communal Body of Christ – the anointed one – and empowers them to live His life on earth as their own. As was already established in Chapter 2, being an extension of the divine life within the human *socium*, the Body of Christ represents the new Christ-like consciousness of the Kingdom that prioritizes the other and their wellbeing.

In view of the above, the immediate theological implication of the unique economic model of the Pentecost community (Acts 2.42-47; 4.34; 5.1-12) expressed in shared ownership of possessions, is the organic ontological and eschatological unity of the faith community with Christ. As Luke T. Johnson points out, 'The sharing of all things was a direct sign of the unity generated by the Spirit; it was a Spirit-filled gesture'.[82] Thus, the life of the first believers 'is the life of the Spirit'.[83] Luke's account of this incarnation of the divine life in the Body of Christ is placed in the context of conversion. Becoming a New Humanity in Christ with a new Christ-like consciousness precedes sharing of material existence. As Johnson concludes, here Luke uses possessions 'as the expression of inner life'.[84] Therefore, the Pentecost community's communal property is a direct outcome of its oneness with Christ and one another by virtue of being His Body. If there is one Christ, there is one Body and

---

[82] Luke T. Johnson, *The Literary Function of Possessions in Luke–Acts* (Missoula, MT: Scholars Press, 1977), p. 208.

[83] Johnson, *The Literary Function of Possessions in Luke–Acts*, p. 185.

[84] Johnson, *The Literary Function of Possessions in Luke–Acts*, p. 184.

a single ownership of its possessions. They are the possessions of Christ Himself – they serve His purpose and mission on earth and are an expression of Christ's self-sharing in His Body. As He overflows into the believers, they overflow into one another in the organic corporal life of the Spirit-filled *koinonia*.

If 'possessions are symbolic expressions of ourselves because we both are and have bodies',[85] then surrendering our possessions to Christ is accepting His identity (and that of His Body) as our own. The Fathers of the Church saw the image of God in humanity as incorporating the totality of the human being – of its spiritual and material existence.[86] Therefore, the likeness of God also cannot exclude the body and its material extension of possessions. Scripture continually emphasizes the reality of the body when articulating the mandate for sanctification (1 Thess. 4.3-8; 5:23, Heb. 9.13-14; Rom. 6.19). The sanctifying work of the Spirit involves the totality of the human existence with all of its social and material expressions in actions, relationships, and desires.

Pentecost and Moral Economic Responsibility

As the Incarnation, so also Pentecost affirms the ontological relationship between matter and Spirit and opens the door to understanding 'the material condition of others as a spiritual matter'.[87]

The economic paradigm of the Pentecost community affirms this understanding and outlines the social responsibilities of holiness as an extension of the life of the Spirit in human flesh. Saintliness manifests itself as serving the material needs of others with one's own possessions. Sharing possessions, therefore, becomes an expression of participation in the life of God and a materialization of shared spirituality.

Edith Wyschogrod offers the following identifier of sainthood:

> A saintly life is defined as one in which compassion for the Other, irrespective of cost to the saint, is a primary trait ... Their

---

[85] Luke T. Johnson, *Sharing Possessions: Mandate and Symbol of Faith* (Philadelphia: Fortress Press, 1981), p. 40.

[86] Lossky, *Orthodox Theology: An Introduction*, p. 71, Stavropoulos, 'Partakers in the Divine Nature', p. 186.

[87] Sallie McFague, 'Epilogue: The Human Dignity and the Integrity of Creation', in Darby Kathleen Ray (ed.), *Theology that Matters: Ecology, Economy and God* (Minneapolis: Fortress Press, 2006), p. 209.

> [the saints'] lives exhibit two types of negation: the negation of self and the lack of what is needful but absent in the life of the Other.[88]

Sallie McFague argues that personal material possessions can blind humanity to the material needs of others as being a spiritual matter. She asserts that 'self-emptying, self-denial, allows us to see differently and hence to live differently ... it is often the first step toward universal love of others, toward seeing others as valuable and all as interrelated'.[89]

Viewed as self-denial on behalf of the others, the acts of sharing possessions stand among the gestures and images that summon our moral response through the hagiographies of the saints as imitators of Christ. Their redeemed humanity is defined not 'by consumption but by *kenosis*' that flows out of 'participation in the fullness of the Trinitarian life' – of mutual self-giving and receiving.[90] As the saints empty themselves in the Body of Christ they become His Body on earth and are transfigured into His New Humanity taking the form and shape of their destiny and mission in Christ-likeness. This imitation is interpreted as a fulfillment of the broader mission of the community of faith – the ministry of reconciliation. The peacemaking of the sons and daughters of God in this world is clearly not limited to the cessation of war and physical violence. It points to shalom of comprehensive justice that involves all humanity and the rest of creation. Therefore, the definition of peace also includes 'providing the earth and its people with the basics of existence',[91] and thus, affirming their dignity and identity as being part of our own common destiny.

The brief Pentecost interruption of the historical economic cycle exposed the profound need for the sanctification of humanity and its desires and pointed to the internal struggle of human consciousness when faced with the vision of the Kingdom in the midst of the temptations and promises of this world's economic systems. As

---

88 Edith Wyschogrod, *Saints and Postmodernity: Revisioning Moral Philosophy* (Chicago: University of Chicago Press, 1990), p. xxi.

89 MacFague, 'Epilogue ... ', pp. 209-10.

90 William T. Cavanaugh, *Being Consumed: Economics and Christian Desire* (Grand Rapids, MI: Eerdmans, 2008), p. 86.

91 MacFague, 'Epilogue ... ', p. 209.

Cavanaugh asserts, our temptation is to spiritualize our union and solidarity with the poor, the oppressed, the suffering …

> … to make our connection to the hungry a sentimental act of imaginative sympathy. We could then even imagine that we are already in a community with those who lack food, whether or not we actually meet their physical needs. We might even wish to tell ourselves that our purchase of consumer goods do in fact feed others – by creating jobs. But we have no way of knowing if such jobs create dignity or merely take advantage of others' desperation … [92]

The tragic story of Ananias and Sapphira (Acts 5.1-10) illustrates this point. Their death could be seen as a sign of the ultimate end of the spirituality behind it – it does not have a future in the Kingdom of God. It is a spirituality that needs redemption and atonement, for the wages of sin is death. Selfishness is contrasted with self-giving; sin is contrasted with saintliness and at the heart of this demarcation are material possessions. Rejecting the needs of others and reconciling one's consciousness with self-centeredness is placed in the context of lying to the community of faith – an act described as lying to the Holy Spirit (Acts 5.9). If the Spirit is the author and internal dynamic of the Pentecost economic model, then falsifying the visible sign of communal unity is 'to falsify the Spirit itself'.[93] That lying to the community of faith is understood as lying to God emphasizes the unity between Christ and His Body. This community is an extension of the life of God on earth; it is the doing and presence of the Spirit in the midst of the human *socium*.

Therefore, economics are a spiritual matter and an external expression of the individual and communal inner life. This is why poverty, as class-related reality, may be viewed as an outcome of a given spirituality that ushers and sustains economic models which maintain and deepen economic gaps and further class-division. This spirituality stands in contrast to the therapeutic measures in the Old and the New Covenants, aimed against further class-dislocation and towards restoring moral economic and civic responsibility in society at large. The concept of Jubilee is a striking example of the demand

---

[92] Cavanaugh, *Being Consumed*, p. 56.

[93] Johnson, *The Literary Function of Possessions in Luke–Acts*, p. 208.

for a social covenant that executes economic justice and sustains human dignity. The forgiveness of debt and restoration of personal freedom are pointers to the spiritual destiny of the covenant people and their social bonds.[94]

The event of Pentecost induces an economic model of distributive justice as a witness of Christ's resurrected life in the Spirit-filled community (Acts 4.32-33). As Marcia Riggs states,

> … corporate good requires sustainability. The means toward sustainability is the sharing of resources – that is distributive justice. Distributive justice means that all have the basics to survive and flourish.[95]

This model is based on reverent consumption, which shares the concern of wellbeing for all (Acts 4.34-35). Historically, Marxist thinkers have questioned the sustainability of this model and have identified the sharing of products without sharing the means of production as the primary reason for its decline and eventual disappearance.[96] The primary issue in the Act's account, however, is concerned with sustainability of unity, human dignity, and love as being the fundamental bonds of the Pentecost social covenant and tangible expression of the participation of the faith community in the communal life of the Trinity.

The pouring of the Spirit on all flesh gives a global dimension to the eschatological vision of Pentecost. All flesh is bonded together in and through the life of the Spirit and made participant in its socio-economic reality. This globalized ethos is indispensable from the anticipation of the planetary spread of the Kingdom of God – the reality of the life of God translated in the socio-political and economic dimensions of material existence on earth. This is a reality in which economics become an outcome and an extension of the divine life through the agency of the Holy Spirit. As such, economics is an extension of justice as the fundamental relationship to the

---

[94] For a study of the Jubilee theme in the Synoptic Gospels and its implication for ethics see Sharon H. Ring, *Jesus, Liberation and the Biblical Jubilee: Images for Ethics and Christology* (Philadelphia: Fortress Press, 1985).

[95] Marcia Y. Riggs, 'The Globalization of Nothing and Creation Ex Nihilo', in Ray (ed.), *Theology that Matters*, p. 148.

[96] Rosa Luxemburg, 'Socialism and the Churches', *Marxist Classics*, http://www.newyouth.com/archives/clssics/luxemburg/socialismandthechurches.html.

other (things and beings). Through the Spirit all flesh is brought into this comprehensive justice that realigns matter with its spiritual origin and purpose. This is a radical transfiguring of the fundamental relationships that construct the human *socium*, moving from material want and desires undergirding production and consumption in the context of anxious awareness of the depletion of material and energy resources to spiritual life that permeates redemptively all material existence and translates it in the comprehensive shalom of the Kingdom. This is life in the Spirit that is more abundant. It is life free from fear and competition for survival – a life in which there is a home for all (Jn 14.2). In it God is the source of all needed for existence and, in contrast to the doom of entropy, He opens the door of all energy and matter, making the horizon of imagination and daydreaming once again available for all. Creative engagement with this openness brings forth visions and dreams into an imaginative envisioning of the world and its future – a day-dreaming inspired by the Spirit Himself.

As was emphasized in Chapter 1, Pentecost reveals the children of God, and their presence on earth is manifested in God's therapeutic justice exercised through them toward creation. Sharing possessions becomes the first sign of this divinely induced reality of healing all creation. It deconstructs the urge to consume and store for consumption; it places human materiality and desires in the perspective of the impossibility to add to one's life through anxiety about the future and the materialization of this anxiety in accumulating material possessions beyond one's immediate existential needs (Lk. 12.15-34).

The Pentecost's community prioritization of searching first for the Kingdom of God has not left even one needy among them (Acts 4.34) – a testimony of the social transformation of material existence when transfigured by its union with the Spirit.

This redemptive eschatological union with God in the Cosmic Christ is both experienced and anticipated in the 'liturgical anamnesis'[97] of the community of faith. The anamnesis of Christ (1 Cor. 11.24-25) is not a mental recollection, but an enacted likeness. It is choosing 'to be' and 'to do' like Him, becoming His extension on

[97] Pfeil, 'Liturgy and Ethics', p. 136.

earth through the incarnational agency of the Holy Spirit. Through the Body of Christ, heaven descends on earth and restores the unity of the Creator with His creation as the liturgical celebration translates the foretaste of the divine fullness of life in and through the Spirit-baptized *koinonia.*

The Eucharist as Pedagogy of Disciplining Desires

The Eucharist is the focal point of the liturgical celebration of Christ's oneness with His Body. As Meeks points out, the Eucharist

> is God's economic act par excellence in the household of Jesus Christ. In it is made present God's own self-giving, God's own economy by which God intends to make the world into a home.[98]

The Eucharist asserts the innocence of the non-anthropic[99] creation which comes to the table of God prior to the human community and welcomes it as the visible form of divine nourishment in the household of God. Through its inclusion within Christ in the act of the incarnation, created matter enters redemptive participation in the life of the Trinity. In the materiality of the Son's body, matter is sanctified and sanctioned as an instrument of grace in the consecration of the cosmos.[100]

The Eucharist provides pedagogy of discerning and liturgical anamnesis of the ontological, soteriological, and eschatological interrelation between humanity and the rest of creation. It instructs us towards disciplining our desires in prioritization of the well-being of others and points us to the practice of liturgical asceticism of reverent consumption (1 Cor. 11.27-34).

The Eucharist effectively deconstructs the logic of free-market consumerism, for as the individual partakes in the Eucharistic elements, she

> does not simply take Christ into her-self, but is taken up into Christ … The act of consumption is thereby turned inside out:

---

[98] Meeks, *God the Economist*, p. 45.

[99] I am using 'non-anthropic' as a synonym to 'not human' in designation of the part of creation that does not incorporate the human *socium* and includes all the rest of the terrestrial created things and beings.

[100] See Chapter 2 of this book.

> instead of simply consuming the body of Christ, we are consumed by it.[101]

As 'we all partake of the one bread' (1 Cor. 10.17) we stand as one Body, for we have all become partakers of Christ and in Him - of each other. Therefore, prioritizing one's personal desires over against the needs of others, and consuming the other for one's own self-gratification within the Body of Christ becomes devouring oneself.

The ultimate challenge of the Eucharistic logic and pedagogy is that by becoming the Body of Christ, we 'must become food for others'.[102] Alexander Schmemann contemplates this extroverted missionary orientation of the Eucharist in reflecting upon the three liturgical movements of its celebration. It starts with a movement of ascent as the Church is carried by the Spirit to heaven in 'its entrance into the new eon'.[103] The church experiences the fullness of the life of the community of the Trinity at the table of the Lord, and being filled and illumined by the divine presence she is called to descend back to earth. This second movement of descent is part of her missiological identity, for unless the Church reenters this world there will not be 'heaven on earth'. Yet, the Church returns on earth for the sake of the world and her final liturgical movement is from the interiority of the temple to the exteriority of all the world – even to its 'uttermost' parts – the farthest, the darkest, the most different from us. Therefore, 'the Eucharist transforms the Church into what it is, transforms it into mission'.[104] In fulfilling her calling, the Church enters the cosmos as the living gospel in the Body of Christ that gives itself daily to feed and heal a starved and broken world.

The Eucharist detoxifies us from the dehumanizing poisons of unrestrained consumerism and helps us to build immunity towards its seductive lure. It cultivates the community of faith as a dissident force of resistance against the commodification of market logic and forms it as an incarnated critique of the utilitarian objectification of God's creation.

---

[101] Cavanaugh, *Being Consumed*, p. 54.
[102] Cavanaugh, *Being Consumed*, p. 55.
[103] Schmemann, 'The Missionary Imperative', p. 200.
[104] Schmemann, 'The Missionary Imperative', p. 200.

In many Eastern European Pentecostal communities the Eucharistic liturgy is followed by an agape feast. While the Eucharist takes place in heaven, the agape feast takes place on earth. It embodies the ultimate purpose of the Eucharistic pedagogy – it is the life of heaven on earth captured by the household table of the family of God where all share their resources and freely receive access to life so that there is not a single one left hungry and needy among them. They are all children in their Father's house and equal beneficiaries of His loving homebuilding on behalf of all of creation.

Many Eastern European Pentecostal communities spend time in fasting prior to celebrating the Eucharist. The believers commit to the fast as part of their spiritual hygiene, cleansing themselves from blind submission to the urge for consumption and learning to differentiate between their legitimate needs and self-indulgent desires. Further, the fast sharpens the believer's spiritual vision, helping them to discern rightly the Body of Christ and to partake in the Lord's Supper in a worthy manner (1 Cor. 11.26-28). It opens his/her eyes to recognize Christ in the other and to embrace them as an organic part of the same family, as members of the same household. The fast prompts the believers to examine their minds and hearts for any negation of Christ expressed as a negation of the other. Therefore, the Eucharist liturgy includes private and public (individual and corporate) confessions and responsive articulation of forgiveness directed towards healing of one's relationship to the other – for, a separation from them is a separation from Christ, from His communal body. The Christoforming work of the Eucharistic liturgy cultivates in the believer the holiness without which no one shall see God (Heb. 12.14). This social holiness that starts with discerning Christ in the other – even in His most radically different and unrecognizable appearance (Mt. 25.31-46) brings the believers face to face with God now, as they share possessions with the other in benevolent actions towards those in need. Therefore, seeing the face of God in the face of the needy on this side of the *eschaton* brings them before His face in eternity as heirs of the Kingdom prepared for them by the Father 'before the foundations of the earth' (Mt. 25.34).

Therefore, the Eucharist transforms the Church into a 'passage' to heaven, 'from the old into the new, from this world into the "world to come"'.[105] It teaches us, as Schmemann points out, that we were created as Eucharistic beings,

> 'as celebrants of the sacrament of life, of its transformation into life in God … We know that real life is 'eucharist', a movement of love and adoration toward God, the movement in which alone the meaning and value of all that exists can be revealed and fulfilled.

This is a powerful antidote to the deformities of the free market's secular liturgies that have distorted our vision of the world. It is a redemptive recapitulation of humanity's economic life into God's economy of household.[106]

Pentecost and the Ecological Economics of Household

Like the non-anthropic Creation, the economic model of Pentecost follows the pattern of sharing versus trading of goods and labor – it follows the pattern of the Creator's self-sharing. The communal composition of the Pentecost model moves from the social-economic predicament of the market to that of the household. The relationships of the household are not based on the amount of capital or possessions the members have, but on their family bonds. In contrast to the market, the household does not produce and maintain class structure. The social position of the members of the household is based upon family roles and any privileges that pertain to these are appropriated within the understanding of mutual calling to one-another as a part of the same family. The members belong to one another: they are each other's brothers, sisters, mothers, children, etc. They are called together in a shared family identity. The family's wealth is the wealth of all its members, who share freely in its benefits. Household material possessions are utilized by the household members for the common benefit of the household unit. The wellbeing of the household as a whole guarantees the wellbeing of all its members. It is not accidental that the family table is the centerpiece of the household and its economic model. It symbolizes sharing of the fundamental necessities of life between equals in identity and purpose. The family is nurtured and sustained

---

105 Schmemann, *For the Life of the World*, p. 31.
106 Schmemann, *For the Life of the World*, p. 34.

as its members break bread together and share possessions – they share life and make life together.

The community of Pentecost as the household of God exhibits this family-like pattern of sharing life which also naturally includes sharing of possessions. Their identity as children of God, born into one family by the same Spirit, outweighs any particularities of gender, ethnicity, and economic class. It establishes instead the dynamic of the traditional family roles, including care-giving, nurture, protection, and provision for the needs of all. The bringing of the members' possessions at the feet of the apostles (Acts 4.32-35) symbolizes their recognition of being called together, belonging together as one family in the household of God

The household of God includes all creation. The household image, therefore, summons to responsibility the members of the family of God to care for creation and its needs. The well-being of the entire household demands this care. The household of God extends beyond the visible and brings together heaven and earth into one Spirit-community. Care, compassion, and love, in the context of recognition of mutual belonging are characteristics of the family bonds in the household.

The response to the other as an act of economic and social justice in Pentecost communal economics is not an outcome of socio-political persuasion but of spirituality that extends one's participation in the life of God and His presence on earth in the community of faith. This spirituality prioritizes the needs and well-being of the other as indispensable from the well-being of the entire household while exercising discernment between personal needs and desires and disciplining ones desires toward the likeness of God. This self-limiting ascetic spirituality stands in a clear contrast to the motives of the secular gestures of one's re-spacing under the legislated and institutionalized forms of redistribution of wealth associated with the capitalist and socialist arrangements discussed earlier in this chapter.

Conclusion

The Pentecost community, as an outcome of the socio-transformative work of the Spirit, becomes the embodiment of God's hospitality and self-sharing with the other within the present (Acts 2.43-47).

This divine hospitality is an all-inclusive justice. It reunites economics with their spiritual foundations in the new Christ-like consciousness of the believers. The consequence is a new form of economic relationships, that is, relationships that embrace the other and provide for their need out of one's own resources. The result is 'having all things in common' (v. 45) and sharing possessions as a visible material expression of the *oikonomia* of God's household. These new economic relations set the Pentecost community apart from the economics of the world. Thus, one encounters in the midst of the world the doing of the Spirit[107] who has birthed the believers into the socio-political reality of God's Kingdom and has transformed them into an extension of that reality on earth. The Spirit is the one who initiates and sustains the conditions that make this radical economic justice possible, for such justice is an outcome of one's act of worship in Spirit and Truth. Therefore, as was proven by the Eastern-European Marxist experiment, the secularization of this vision is destined to failure.

Breaking bread together (v. 46) as both daily commensality and Eucharistic celebration of the unity of the Body of Christ becomes a symbolic centerpiece of living out the just socio-political reality of the Kingdom within the household of God.[108] As Brian Blount

---

[107] Miroslav Volf, *Exclusion and Embrace: A Theological Exploration of Identity, Otherness, and Reconciliation* (Nashville: Abingdon Press, 1996), pp. 228-29. For an extensive study on the spiritual mandate of sharing possessions, see Johnson, *Sharing Possessions*. The author discusses the topic also in relation to the event of Pentecost (p. 21).

[108] In her book *Of Widows and of Meals: Communal Meals in the Book of Acts* (Grand Rapids, MI: Eerdmans, 2007), Reta Halterman Finger offers an in-depth study of the daily commensality of natural and fictive kin groups in first-century Palestine. She examines the passages in Acts concerning the economic life of the early Christians on the background social economic practices of the day and from the contextual viewpoint of the poor (especially widows and their daughters who were one of the most economically destitute demographic groups). She emphasizes the communal daily breaking of bread both as sharing between kin in a communal eating as well as a sacramental practice the origination of which is in the meals Jesus shared with both Jews and Gentiles. Some authors have distinguished between the *koinonia* in Acts 2.42 and the breaking of bread as between communal and Eucharistic meals. However, it is the presence of Jesus Christ that transforms a meal into a Lord's Supper. Therefore, the sacramental nature of sharing the meal in the name of the Lord in evocation of His presence in the unity of His Body on earth in thanksgiving is translated in both daily commensality and the Eucharist.

points out, 'The first-century, Palestinian table symbolized much more than a meal; it was a representation of community'.[109] Jesus had already extended the hospitality of God to the Gentiles, inviting them around the table of God in the feeding of the four thousand in the region of Decapolis (Mk 8.1-10) – he had 'offered the bread of God's table to people of all nations'.[110]

Likewise, the Pentecost community as the Body of the risen Christ continues His ministry of self-sharing hospitality to a starved and destitute humanity. Under the Messianic anointing of the Spirit, the community of Christ is empowered daily to follow the Lord who gives His broken body so that others may live. Through the incarnational agency of the Spirit, the Pentecost community becomes an extension of this Messianic self-giving and lays down its bruised and broken Body as a table where the nations can come and feast freely. After they have tasted the Lord, nothing else may satisfy their hunger. In anticipation of the socio-transformative 'Christification' of the cosmos,[111] the community of faith manifests God's presence as a prophetic critique of the consciousness and economic relations in the world, exposing their conflict with the ultimate destiny of humanity. Beyond the historical horizon stands the cosmic Christ as the summation of all things in heaven and on earth[112] – facing the present with the inevitability of its future.

The current philosophical crossroads of the Eastern European context reflect its dichotomization between ideological nostalgia for the predictable past and its present socio-political metamorphosis, attempting to meet the demands of global existence under the pressure of a capitalist market economy. As the Eastern European countries face the trivialization of utopia in their contemporary post-communist setting, they struggle to formulate a viable paradigm for social transformation capable of sustaining and navigating

---

[109] Brian K. Blount, 'The Apocalypse of Worship: A House of Prayer for all Nations', in Brian K. Blount and Leonora Tubbs Tisdale (eds.) *Making Room at the Table: An Invitation to Multicultural Worship* (Louisville, Kentucky: Westminster John Knox Press, 2001), p. 20.

[110] Blount, 'The Apocalypse of Worship', p. 21.

[111] Moltmann, *Jesus Christ for Today's World*, p. 101. As stated earlier, Moltmann picks up the idea of cosmic evolving towards Christ from Teilhard de Chardin's 'Christ the Evolver' in *Christianity and Evolution.*

[112] Tutu, *No Future without Forgiveness*, p. 265.

their journey towards a new socio-political identity of global citizenship.

The Eastern European civilization stands upon dozens of centuries of institutional Christianity. Yet today, it is more materialistic and self-absorbed than ever before. The crowds at the Orthodox temples, driven by spiritual hunger and yet disappointed by the Church's social inadequacy and compromised integrity, cluster around the Easter candles in hope for a social communal resurrection. What can theology offer to these generations, broken and bruised by an oppressive history, uprooted and displaced in a fragmented, antagonized, and disillusioned world after the desacralization of ideals and profanation of dreams?

The biblical vision of Pentecost communal economics offers precisely the type of challenge to the socio-political imagination needed in this part of the world. After fifty years of living in the nightmare of its distorted secular version, perhaps it is time for society to find a renewed inspiration in its original paradigm for social transformation. It offers an ideological model that reunites economics with their spiritual foundations in the Christ-like consciousness of the believers. The result is a new form of economic relationships, that is, relationships that embrace the other and prioritize their well-being as an extension of God's self-sharing with His world. Perhaps the Pentecost vision of radical inclusion of all God's creatures in His comprehensive socio-economic justice is precisely the ideological substance that can birth hope within a hope-depleted context awaiting the social redemption of its economic life on this side of eschatology.

4

The City of Humanity and the City of God: Pentecost, Hospitality, and the Redemption of Culture

Origins and Nature of the Human City

Scripture places the origins of the city and, thus, the dawn of human civilization in the shocking drama of fratricide (Gen. 4.1-17). Reflecting on the disturbing genesis of the earthly city in his timeless masterpiece, *The City of God*, St. Augustine contrasts the story's protagonists, Abel and Cain, as the citizens of two rivaling realities – the City of God and the city of humanity. He sees this primordial account of shedding brotherly blood as the archetype for the founding of Rome, destined to become the center of human civilization, 'the capital of that earthly city'.[1] Yet, Augustine differentiates between the conflict of Remus and Romulus and that of Abel and Cain by describing them as symptomatic of two different realities. According to him, the first pair exemplifies the division existing within the human city, the second, the enmity between the earthly and the heavenly cities.[2] As in the parable of the man who sows good seed in his field only to be contaminated with tares by his enemy (Mt. 13.24-30), Augustine sees the two cities as existing side by side until the last judgment – the separation of those destined for

---

[1] St. Augustine, *City of God* (trans. G.G. Walsh, D.B. Zema, G. Monahan and D.J. Honnan; New York: Doubleday, 1958), p. 328.

[2] St. Augustine states, 'Thus, we have two wars, that of the wicked at war with the wicked and that of the wicked at war with the good. For, of course, once the good are perfectly good, there can be no war between them' (*City of God,* p. 329).

eternal life from those destined for eternal punishment. Until that day, the City of God 'lives like an alien inside' the city of humanity.[3] While the earthly city originates with the offspring of the first Adam in the conditions of fallen human nature, Christ – the last Adam, the first fruit of the new humanity – is the founder of the heavenly city, the Church,[4] which endures persecution, negation, and ridicule within the walls of the earthly city.[5] Yet she is the very nugget of the life to come – the seed of heaven on earth, the future of true human flourishing visible in 'the peace of the heavenly city' that takes the form of 'ordered and harmonious communion of those who find their joy in God and in one another in God'.[6]

Built on aggression of one human being against another, for Augustine the earthly city is incapable of securing true peace. Its violent ontogenesis self-perpetuates in a vicious cycle of strife and conflict that makes the harmonious co-existence of humanity an ever-distant illusion. 'The City of God, however, has a peace of its own, namely, peace with God in this world by faith and in the world to come by vision'.[7] Ultimately, for Augustine, God is the true life of humanity[8] and those who are in peace with God here and now have access to life, and live life more abundant. The ones who are divorced from God are severed from life and walk on a path of death that starts in this age and crosses into eternity.

Reaching beyond Augustine's interpretation, we can see in the story of Abel and Cain a symbolic summary of a profound civilizational shift in human history. As John Dominic Crossan suggests, in this inaugural fratricide that marks the invention of human civilization, the farmer kills the shepherd and builds a city, or rather, the farmer displaces the shepherd[9] as sedentary culture replaces nomadic life.

Consequently, the theme of the tension between sedentary and nomadic existence reappears over and over again in the biblical narrative as a subtle nuance of God's salvific history with humanity.

---

[3] Augustine, *City of God*, p. 391.
[4] Augustine, *City of God*, p. 385.
[5] Augustine, *City of God*, p. 419.
[6] Augustine, *City of God*, p. 456.
[7] Augustine, *City of God*, p. 480.
[8] Augustine, *City of God*, p. 479.
[9] Crossan, *God and Empire*, pp. 60-61.

Thus, in the story of Babel, God's redemptive intervention comes as deconstruction of the settled hierarchical concentration of control over economic, ideological, military, and political resources[10] (as human control over fellow humans) and the reversal of the civilizations' violent urbanization into a journey away from the valley of Shinar, towards the face of the unknown, towards the frontiers of the earth.

In the post-flood account of the re-initiated human civilization we witness also God calling Abraham (then still Abram) out of his native country and his father's house, out of the safety and predictable familiarity of one's urban culture on a journey to another, unknown land (Gen. 12.1). Yet, Abraham remains nomad even in the promised land of Canaan – a choice contrasted with that of his nephew Lot,[11] seduced by the prosperity and false promise of security within the walls of the city (Gen. 13.12; 14.12). Like the project of Babel, Lot represents the drama of humanity within 'the cage'[12] of human civilization (itself an expression of longing for peace and safety and of the attempt to realize these goals through the homog-

---

[10] According to Michael Mann, these are the four principle sources of social power the concentration of which mark the origins of human civilization. See Michael Mann, *The Sources of Social Power*, vol. I (New York: Cambridge University Press, 1986).

[11] Genesis chapters 18 (the story of the hospitality of Abraham to the three divine visitors) and 19 (the hospitality of Lot to the strangers who have come as God's messengers of forthcoming judgment upon the city of Sodom) are often compared and contrasted in relation to their structure and content as are Abraham and Lot themselves. While, to my knowledge, they have not been contrasted in terms of the theme of tension between sedentary and nomadic existence and its symbolic implications, there are a number of texts that offer valuable insights within the literary and theological significance of the stories' parallelism. See, for example, Victor P. Hamilton, *The Book of Genesis: Chapters 18-50* (Grand Rapids, MI: Eerdmans, 1995), pp. 28-54; Wilbur Glenn Williams, *Genesis: A Bible Commentary in the Wesleyan Tradition* (Indiana, IN: Wesleyan Publishing House, 2000), pp. 152-59; and Gerhard von Rad, *Genesis* (trans. John H. Mark; Philadelphia: The Westminster Press, 1961), pp. 210-17.

[12] Mann, *The Sources of Social Power*. Mann uses the metaphor of 'a social cage' or 'the cage' as a designation of human civilization (p. 38). He states that 'civilization combines three social institutions, the ceremonial center, writing and the city', thus inaugurating 'a jump in human collective power over nature and over other humans'. This process involves territorial retention and social stratification, 'caging' the population 'into particular authority relations' (p. 124). Within this arrangement, religion became 'society stretched "ideally to the stars". As society became caged, so did religion' (p. 47).

enizing compression of urbanization). At the destruction of Sodom, Lot has to flee the city and find refuge in nature – an act of migration out of the creation of humanity back into the creation of God. Still, he tries to negotiate another option for urban existence in the settlement of (what becomes known as) Zoar (Gen. 19.19-20) – a wish graciously granted by God (Gen. 19.21), perhaps in recognition that the city is in Lot even when he is out of the city.[13] The human project has become inseparable from human identity.

Even in the face of imminent danger, Lot is reluctant to leave the walls of Sodom. Therefore, we read:

> But he hesitated. So the men seized his hand and the hand of his wife and the hands of his two daughters, for the compassion of the Lord was upon him; and they brought him out, and put him outside the city (Gen. 19.16).

The compassion of God extracts Lot from the city and guides him towards the refuge of nature (Gen. 19.17). The angels point to the mountains as the place of true safety from the upcoming disaster (Gen. 19.17). In Lot's imagination, however, nature is associated with ever-present danger (v. 19) – an association reminiscent of Babel's imperial propaganda cultivating fear of the unknown outside of the city walls – fear of the other.[14] Perhaps, in his moment of

---

[13] Perhaps the most vivid expression of the volatile symbiosis between human identity and urban existence is exemplified by the story of Lot's wife. Her turning back to look at Sodom joins her end to that of the city. The inherent movement of return that is reminiscent in her turning back could be viewed as symbolic of the orientation of her heart and desires, of the content of her longings and self-identification with the dreams of this human civilization now standing under judgment. Sodom represents a reality that has no future in the just providence of God, and so too are the ones who have allied themselves with it. Sharing in the dreams of the city (its vision of the good life) means sharing in its ends. The classical interpretations offered regarding the morphing of Lot's wife into a pillar of salt look at her action of turning back as a direct defiance of the order given by the messengers (v. 17): e.g. Hamilton, *The Book of Genesis*, p. 48. There are, however, more creative interpretations that look at the event as 'a monument' to the 'perils of inertia' that can paralyze us in the face of danger and cause us to act against our God-given survival instincts. See Naomi H. Rosenblatt and Joshua Horwitz, *Wrestling With Angels: What the First Family of Genesis Teaches Us About Our Spiritual Identity, Sexuality, and Personal Relationships* (New York: Delacorte Press, 1995), pp. 180-81.

[14] Rosenblatt and Horwitz point out that 'Our primal fear of the unknown speaks to our subconscious fear of the other' (*Wrestling with Angels*, p. 173). The

personal drama, Lot represents human alienation from nature, a loss of humanity's way as part of God's creation in its origin and destiny, and its surrender to self-destructive, dehumanizing lifestyle – an illustration of the negative effects of civilization contrasted with God's provision for true human flourishing (authentic community with God and in Him with one's neighbor). The violently unnatural behavior of Sodom's male citizens further illustrates the debasing state of humanity away from its divinely ordained purpose as God's creature (vv. 4-9). In its alienation and perversion, Sodom's civilization bends nature towards its distortion and annihilation. Humanity brings about its end by losing its natural identity – it ceases to exist according to its creaturely design and thus, its physical self-extinction becomes just a matter of time. The pattern of self-destruction takes the form of violence towards the other for one's own self-indulgence. The other becomes a disposable commodity – they are objectified and defaced in an uncontrollable urge for personal gratification. They are dehumanized by the abusers that force them in degrading, unnatural behavior, which denies them the dignity and respect of free moral agents.

The violent coercive commodification within human civilization that turns humanity against its nature and purpose finds its ultimate expression in alienation from God and fellow humans. Thus, the human city appears over and over again as a symbol of opposition

---

authors reflect on Genesis 19 in light of this statement and the conviction that 'Part of the price of urban violence is our growing reluctance to extend even common courtesy to strangers' (p. 174). They discuss 'the sins of Sodom' in terms of injustice and violence against the other (pp. 177-78). In relation to the judgment of the city, the authors assert that 'a society's fate is ultimately determined by its moral and social behavior' (p. 179). Von Rad points out that while 'Sodom was always the example of greatest depravity that one could think of in Israel ... the notion about the particular nature of its sin was not always the same. Isaiah seems to have considered it the barbarity of their administration of justice (Isa. 1.10; 3.9); Ezekiel, however, thinks of 'pride, surfeit of food, and prosperous ease' (Ezek. 16.49); and Jeremiah speaks of adultery, lying, and unwillingness to repent (Jer. 23.14)' (*Genesis*, p. 213). Thus, von Rad highlights the complexity of the utilization of Sodom's metaphorical significance in Israel's ethical tradition. Alongside Rosenblatt and Horowitz, John Goldingay focuses on the violent oppression exercised by the city towards the other. He sees Sodom as 'a small scale version of the world itself on the eve of the flood, in the pervasiveness of its wickedness and in the nature of that wickedness as involving ... violence and especially sexual violence' (*Old Testament Theology*, vol. I, *Israel's Gospel* [Downers Grove, IL: InterVarsity Press, 2003], p. 229).

to the divine plan for redemption of humanity, perhaps most notoriously so in the image of 'Babylon the great' in the Book of Revelation (Rev. 14.8; 16.19; 17.5; 18.2, 10, 21). The judgment against her is the final judgment of human civilization – a negation of all its vices and corruption. The fall of the city is the outcome of its violent conflict with God and His servants which brings to an end Babylon's false sense of safety, seductive glamor, prosperity, and pseudo-community (Rev. 18.21-24).

Yet, amidst the negativity associated with the image of the city as a human social project, there is a sense of deep ontological necessity that magnetizes humanity toward the city's domain. In light of the biblical account of creation, perhaps we can look at the historical precedent of the city's construct as an outcome of humanity's natural gravity towards the cultivation of human community – a primordial sense of one's ontological need of his/her fellow human in order to complete one's own humanness. Thus, the city could be viewed as an instinctual expression of humanity's inherent calling to human community. However, outside of God's Trinitarian proto-communal reality as the originator and sustainer of authentic communal life, the communal motive of the city's existence remains an unattainable utopia. Being initiated by violence as an underlying pattern of relation to the other, the city becomes a mere counterfeit of human community. Its fundamental mode of existence is not of belonging together but of alienation from God and neighbor.

The paradoxical nature of the city is exemplified by its walls[15] – a symbol of both inclusion and exclusion, of belonging and separation. Generated by fear from the other, the city builds walls of exclusion and protection against outsiders – walls that simultaneously, however, become 'a cage' for those within separating them from the rest of humanity. As Ronald Wright remarks, 'people afraid of others are easily manipulated' and persuaded to surrender their equality and rights to those who promise them protection, thus,

---

[15] According to Mann, the city walls of the city-state 'symbolized and actualized the cage of authoritative power … one accepted this state and its military commander'. He states: 'The gigantic protection racket of political history began: Accept my power, for I will protect you from worse violence – of which I can give you a sample, if you don't believe me' (*The Source of Social Power*, p. 100).

creating in a sense 'protection racketeers'.[16] Continuing this line of thought, Crossan states that,

> From the beginning, then, civilization became imperial as it attempted to expand social power as mastery over other people through an ever-widening circle of security. It would only be a question, at any given time or place, of who had lost, who had gained, and who still wanted imperial control over others.[17]

Creating and perpetuating inequality and exclusion for the sake of safety, the city construct sabotages the possibility of true human community. Social stratification displaces the face of the fellow human (created to mirror and shape our own humanness) to a designated level within a hierarchy of authority and influence over others that reduces them into utility for securing one's own safety and affluence. Inequality, then, becomes the pathology of human civilization that jeopardizes, degrades, and even on occasion denies humanness to the other thus, deforming humanness in all.

Fear (itself a manifestation of the alienation from God and neighbor)[18] becomes the fuel of this dehumanizing effect of civilizational development and political manipulation its main vehicle. Perhaps this is why Hermann Göring's remarks in an interview from his jail cell at Nürnberg while standing trial for crimes against humanity during WWII sound so deeply disturbing and yet familiar to the North-Atlantic political sensibility:

> ... it is the leaders of a country that determine the policy ... whether it is a democracy or a fascist dictatorship or a Parliament or a Communist dictatorship ... The people can always be brought to the bidding of the leaders. That is easy. All you have

---

[16] Ronald Wright, *A Short History of Progress* (New York: Avalon, 2004), p. 49.

[17] Crossan, *God and Empire*, p. 32.

[18] Discussing the dialectic between alienation, fear, and violence against fellow humans, Nikolas Berdyaev states: 'Fear and slavery are cancerous in their consequences. If the human succeeds to overcome the slavish fear, he (she) will stop killing. The human being sows death out of his (her) fear of death. (Human) Lordship always needs to murder. Lordship always feels fear, and because of that needs to murder. It does not want to fight with death.' The fear of those who rule over others is undergirded by the conviction that if they do not exert power over their fellow humans, someone else will rule over them (*О Робстве и Свободе Человека* [Paris: YMCA - Press, 1939], p. 209).

> to do is tell them they are being attacked and denounce the pacifist for lack of patriotism and exposing the country to danger. It works the same way in any country.[19]

Journeying in and with God

In the subtly nuanced tension between the sedentary and nomadic lifestyle within its narrative, Scripture utilizes the metaphor of a journey with God as descriptive of the formative pedagogy of true faith and right worship and as depiction of the personal and communal experience of transformation into the divine likeness.[20] Faith is described as a pilgrimage out of the earthly city to the city 'whose architect is God' (Heb. 11.10), out of one's native country to the Kingdom of heaven (Heb. 11.16). The believers are characterized as aliens, strangers, and sojourners (1 Pet. 2.11) passing through on a voyage to a different world seeded in this present age as the smallest of seeds (Mt.13.31). The journey defies the physical constrains of time and space evoking the invisible into the visible and manifesting the fruit of the Spirit into the material reality of everyday life, making it a sanctuary of the divine presence. Journeying in the Way within the transformative flow of the Spirit shapes the believers into the Way. They take the embodied form of the One in whom they move and live and have their being – the form of Christ. As they ascend in Christ to heavenly places, He advents in them on earth, bringing to it His Kingdom in the redeemed human community. In the Christoformed believers heaven descends on earth and transfigures it into its likeness. They become like the very Spirit who births them (Jn 3.6b), carries and sustains them on the journey, teaching them to live not with bread alone but with every word that comes from the mouth of God (Mt. 4.4) so that they may learn to nurture others also. The Spirit flows from their innermost

---

[19] Quoted in Crossan, *God and Empire*, p. 36.

[20] From the stories of Enoch (Gen. 5.22) and Noah (Gen. 6.9-8) walking with God, through the journeys of Abraham and the nation of Israel (Abraham's seed – his collective multigenerational representation within the covenant) to the promised land, to Jesus being 'the Way' (Jn 14.4) (a designation later used for His followers – Acts 9.2; 19.9, 23; 22.4; 24.14, 22), Scripture uses the language of travel to depict the journey of faith.

being like rivers of living water (Jn 7.38-39) becoming the very substance of their core.

Thus, becoming like God is a journey in and with the Spirit. Indeed, this journey is in the very ontogenesis of Israel as God's chosen instrument 'to prepare the world for the coming of the Messiah'.[21] They travel with the Spirit, journeying throughout the desert with the pillar of fire by night and the cloud by day – a journey that makes them His people as He becomes their shepherd, guiding, protecting, and providing for their flourishing. Moving with God becomes their daily routine – they learn to watch and wait for the movement of the Spirit and to be prepared to follow. They move when God moves and rest when He rests. They follow His will embodying it in the shape of their journey. This is how it is with the ones who are born of the Spirit (Jn 3.5-8) in the last Adam, who came to do the will of the Father restoring freedom to humanity. They learn to move with and in Him, in the organic harmony of His Body until He is all in all within them.

God extracts Israel from Egypt, from the dehumanizing violence and enslavement of imperial civilization and places them on the nomadic paths of the wilderness where they depend on Him alone for sustenance and safety. This undomesticated, nomadic God who defies the court deities of Pharaoh, unmoved by the political expediency of the imperial agenda, chooses the slaves and lives among them teaching them once again to be free. He walks them throughout the desert until the empire and slavery leave them as they leave slavery and empire.

The pedagogy of journeying with, in, and through God that we see in the synchronized movement of the people of Israel with the Shekinah in the wilderness of Sinai reminds us of another striking vision of the divine presence. No other passage depicts this traveler God more vividly than the first chapter of the Book of Ezekiel. As the heavens open (Ezek. 1.1) unveiling the spiritual realm, making it visible and tangibly present, the prophet sees the throne of God on living, all-seeing wheels moving as the Spirit moves (vv. 15-21). Its breathtaking otherness and complexity is beautifully harmonious, organically cohesive, and glorious. God moves with His celestial

---

[21] Schmemann, *For the Life of the World*, p. 25.

creatures as one integral whole for His Spirit is in them as 'their spirit is in the wheels'. God moves together with, in, and through His invisible celestial creation as it manifests and proclaims His glory. This is how it should be with the visible creation as well. When humanity does not move with its Creator it ends up in slavery and exile; when it does – it becomes like Christ – the hypostatic union of God and humanity in one eternal movement of cosmic healing and renewal.[22]

Yet, the nomad God who dwells and moves about in a tent (2 Sam. 7.2, 6) and cannot be contained by any structure built by human hands (1 Kings 8.27), whose omnipresence permeates all the universe (Ps. 139.7-10), conditionally surrenders to humanity's desire to grow roots and settle down upon a portion of the earth. He stays with His people whom He has shepherded through trials and tribulations in the drama of history-making and nation-building even when they had abandoned Him and disowned him as their Lord. God accepts the building of a temple as a designated sacred place for an encounter with His people. However, He differentiates Himself from violence and bloodshed of one human being against another (1 Chron. 29.3) and appoints a person of peace to build His temple, for His dwelling place is to be a house of prayer for all nations, a place that unites humanity in its diversity, and heals the broken human community, a place where all are at home and have access to life, for all of humanity is His offspring (Acts 17.28).

In a gesture of transgenerational hospitality, in response to David's desire to build Him a house, God establishes the house of David as an everlasting dynasty (2 Sam. 6.11-16). The foundational promise for this living house is the parent-child relationship that binds lovingkindness and correction in guiding the family of God (vv. 14-15). In all of this human-house-building, God's children (His household) are to be His temple on earth – His Spirit is to live in them as they walk in the commandments and ordinances of the

---

[22] For a rich, inspiring interpretation of Ezekiel's vision in the context of the rest of the book see Rickie D. Moore, '"They will know that a prophet has been among them": The Source and End of the Call of Ezekiel', in S.J. Land, R.D. Moore, and J.C. Thomas (eds.), *Passover, Pentecost and Parousia: Studies in Celebration of the Life and Ministry of R. Hollis Gause* (JPTSup 35; Blandford Forum: Deo Publishing, 2010), pp. 53-64.

Lord (1 Chron. 21.7-8). They are to walk with Him as He moves in them. In them God builds His home for all creation.

Beyond the complex socio-political and economic reasons for this compromise with sedentary existence, one particular motive overtakes the logic of the argument for designation of a concrete place for worship to God, namely the challenge of upholding a monotheistic religious experience amidst a polytheistic world.

In its liturgical essence,[23] humanity is designed to worship what it loves and to become what it worships. Therefore, the believers are instructed to love God with the entirety of their being (Mk 12.30; Mt. 22.37; Deut. 6.5) so that they may worship Him alone. Undivided love for God directs all worship towards Him so that the worshiper may be shaped by that worship into the divine likeness until he/she is one with God – until he/she loves what God loves, sees the other person as God sees them, and acts towards them as God does. This is why idolatry is so dangerous for humanity, because worshiping something other than God shapes the human being into something else than God. Idolatry deforms humanity into something less than its calling. It prevents the fulfillment of its *telos* as God's creature. It is dehumanizing. Therefore, worshiping other gods destroys humanity as the temple of God on earth – it desecrates His sanctuary; that is, the image of the Creator in humanity is threatened by distortion beyond recognition. The way to repair this temple is to uproot humanity from its spiritual destruction by placing it back on a corrective/transformative journey with the Spirit – even when this journey is an exile away from the land of the promise. Thus, the believer can experience the place of exile as a place of blessing, healing, and restoration being reminded that human flourishing is not a function of geographical location and natural resources but of the divine presence – of God's loving kindness and gracious hospitality.

Therefore, going back to the vision of Ezekiel of this ever-moving God, undomesticated, unsettled, and unsettling, we see the divine presence evacuating the temple and the city of Jerusalem (Ezekiel 1-8). Idolatry has brought the spiritual desecration of

[23] For an articulation of the human being as a liturgical creature see James K.A. Smith, *Desiring the Kingdom: Worship, Worldview, and Cultural Formation* (Grand Rapids, MI: Baker Academic, 2009), pp. 39-76.

God's house and He announces to the prophet His departure: 'I will go far from my sanctuary' (Ezek. 8.6) – a statement followed later by the promise to become a sanctuary for those displaced in exile (1.16).[24] God defies the religious expectations and challenges the religious imagination remaining unpredictable, incomprehensible, and indefinable. The city and its temple built with human hands are destroyed and with them the sense of certainty of a religious cult settled in the familiarity of predictable sedentary existence and routinization of worship. Instead, God inaugurates a new journey for His people that ends with the gift of a new heart and a new spirit (Ezek. 11.9). God is going to build His temple with living stones (1 Pet. 2.5). He is going to build it in His people who will worship Him in Spirit and Truth (Jn 4.23), moving about with and in God wherever He leads them. This is the end of sacred geography linked to a mystical cult towards the God of Israel. The Body of Christ – the Church – the new people of God gathered in Him remains the only real temple on earth.[25]

It is not accidental that the Church as the City of God comes on earth at the end of time from heaven. To become a temple of the Holy Spirit on earth, the believers first 'must ascend to heaven where Christ has ascended'.[26] After all, they are His disciples because they are the ones who follow Him. Heaven in a human body – Christ Himself – is the destination of their faith journey. He is the one true temple for in Him the fullness of the deity dwells. In him heaven embraces the earth in order to transfigure it into its likeness. He is the high priest who hallows the world by cleansing it with his blood and taking it to the Holy of Holies. In the ascension of the incarnated and resurrected body of the Son of Man who has overcome sin and the grave, He takes the world to heaven and presents it to the Father in the fullness of its perfected form in which Christ is all in all. Thus, redemption becomes a movement of ascent in, with, and towards God – a Christoforming journey from glory to glory in which the Church fulfills her destiny of becoming one with 'the One in whom all things are at their end, and all things are at

---

[24] Moore, 'They will know that a prophet has been among them,' p. 60.
[25] Schmemann, *For the Life of the World*, p. 20.
[26] Schmemann, *For the Life of the World*, p. 28.

their beginning'.[27] In Him the moment of one's *telos* becomes the moment of transfiguring into one's *novum*. Therefore, the redemptive perfecting of history by its summation in Christ as the end of all things, transforms it into a new beginning – the renewal of all things out of decay into life eternal. The old things have passed away and the transfigured world begins anew as new heaven, new earth, and new city. The church that has been called out/summoned from the earth in order to be transformed into heaven, descends as heaven on earth. In heaven she is transfigured into 'the world to come' and as such fulfills her journey towards God and His Kingdom by becoming His Kingdom on earth. The ascent of the Church to heaven has made her God's temple on earth in which the fullness of the Godhead dwells. She has been transformed into a sanctuary and seeded on earth so that the entire world may become a sanctuary.

Redemption and the Other

The narrative of the Tower of Babel (Gen. 11.1-9) outlines the procession of human civilization from localized homogeneity to globalized cultural multiplicity. According to its story, the monolithic project of the human city is deconstructed and dispersed throughout the face of the earth making human civilization a cosmopolitan reality. Within this divinely induced process of globalization, human language becomes the iconic identifier of cultural identity and distinction, the immediate audible marker of cultural diversity. Language becomes the summoning announcement of a new social reality – the appearance of the other. The sudden confusion of languages exposes the fragility of human civilization conditioned by the always-present potentiality of misunderstanding and intercultural conflict.

Indeed, after Babel, language functions as the outlining frontier of a given social group, as the demarcation of a distinct cultural construct/pattern within the vastly diverse human tapestry. Yet, with all of its cultural particularity, language remains a universal marker of humanity and of humanness itself, pointing toward the

---

[27] Schmemann, *For the Life of the World*, p. 27.

social core of the human being as a communal creature reflecting the image of the Social Creator – the proto-community of the Trinity.[28]

At Babel, the breaking down of the monolingual human homogeneity into polyglotic multiculturality brings forth the need of redeeming culture both in its particularity (as a signifier of human diversity) and in its universality (as a universal characteristic of humanity).[29] For indeed, if Babel's deconstruction expresses God's providential action of creating the conditions for the existence of the other as necessity for the redemption of humanity, then it also points to the need of redeeming diversity in multiculturality – redeeming human culture/s.

Therefore, the story of Babel affirms multiculturalism as a necessary predicate to human redemption, as the condition for sustaining true human identity manifested in an organic communal unity of diversity. The restoration of this identity of diversity in singularity – of both the multiplicity and universality of human culture (of the diversity of human cultures in the singularity of humanness), becomes an expression of redemption as healing and restoration of the image and likeness of God in humanity. Only a Creator that exhibits this unique identity (the impossible possibility) of diversity in singularity (or oneness), can become its sustainer, redeemer, and sanctifier in humanity. Thus, the social Trinity is the One and Only God Who can redeem the multiplicity of cultures bringing them together in an organic oneness while sustaining their ethnographic uniqueness. It takes the proto-community of the Trinity to redeem the multiculturality of humanity into one organic global human community. In her perichoretic identity, the Trinity negates any homogenizing force that attempts to coerce human diversity into an easily manageable uniformity. It takes a stand against the impulse of the fallen human nature towards eliminating the inconvenience of the other's existence. It sustains the conditions for the preservation

---

[28] See the comments regarding the translatability of languages as a sign that all humanity is called to one speech community in Chapter 1 of the present book.

[29] For more on the universality and particularity of culture see Kathryn Tenner, *Theories of Culture: A New Agenda for Theology* (Minneapolis, MN: Fortress Press, 1997), pp. 25-27.

and flourishing of the other, apart from whom redemption is impossible.

The Orthodox tradition describes the *perichoresis* of the communal Trinity as 'three divine persons united with one another in the unceasing movement of mutual love'.[30] Redemption makes humanity partaker in this divine communal life (2 Pet. 1.4), placing the human creature under the gentle carving flow of this all-engulfing love until it has been re-created into the perfect embodied image of God – the image of Christ – for 'to be human is to be Christlike',[31] the perfect image of God in human flesh (Col. 1.15). Attaining Christlikeness is restoration of authentic human freedom to be and to become, to love and to be loved. Yet, in accordance with the Trinitarian communal image in humanity, as H.A.H Bartholomew asserts, this true freedom is 'never solitary but always social'.

> We are only free if we become a *prosopon* – to use the Greek word for 'person', which means literally 'face' or 'countenance' – only if we turn towards others, looking into their eyes and allowing them to look into ours. To turn away, to refuse to share, is to forfeit liberty. Freedom is expressed as encounter.[32]

God's redemptive deconstructive action at Babel turns humanity's face towards the other making him/her an unavoidable encounter with the image of God. The centrifugal effect of globalizing human dispersion to the unknown otherness of the 'face of the earth' does not eliminate the inevitability of encounter. Escape from the other is an impossible project, an ever-drifting mirage. The earth's spherical form guides the human journey back face to face with the other denying the possibility for infinite distance. The saving grace of God leads humanity back to the beginning, to the encounter of the face – the image of God facing itself in the other until a person sees oneself in the other as in a mirror and thus, is capable to love the other as oneself (Lev. 19.18, Mt. 19.19). The human journey back to God becomes pedagogy of discerning Him in the other. Apart of seeing God's image in the other one cannot

---

[30] H.A.H. Bartholomew I, Archbishop of Constantinople and Ecumenical Patriarch, *Encountering the Mystery* (New York: Doubleday, 2008), p. 133.

[31] Bartholomew I, *Encountering the Mystery*, p. 132.

[32] Bartholomew I, *Encountering the Mystery*, p. 132.

see God. Apart from loving the other one cannot love God (1 Jn 4.20). Salvation becomes a way of seeing God disguised in the body and face of the other despite their socio-economic, cultural, ethnographic, racial, gender, and language otherness. Thus, the process of discerning Christ in the other, even in his/her most distressful condition (Mt. 25.31-46), becomes the Christoforming power in one's life that ultimately allows one to see God. Seeing Christ in the other makes one like Christ. Each human being stands in the face of the other imprinted with the same origin and destiny – Christ – the beginning and the end – the summation of human civilization in its redeemed form. In this sanctified/deified perspective the face of the other meets us as the future of the world, as the full potentiality of the fullness of life more abundant in, with and through God. There is no future and no salvation without the other.

Recapitulating All in Christ: The Incarnation and Redemption of Human Culture

Redemption and sanctification, as inter-social enterprises of divine grace, point to human identity as a complex social construct of relationships to the other.[33] Therefore, the way of redemption becomes the journey of recapitulating all of these relationships back into the restored ontological communion between humanity and God as the Ultimate Other. The restoration/healing of this fundamental dimension of authentic humanness translates itself into all other social encounters comprising one's identity. Communion with God

---

[33] In his essay 'The Ego and Totality', Emmanuel Levinas reflects on the dialectic between interiority and exteriority of personal identity and the rise of what he terms 'the first thought' beginning 'with the possibility of conceiving freedom external to one's own' (p. 28). This process takes place at the relational boundaries between us and others. Levinas highlights the reality of moral myopia resulting in an innocent violence towards the other (p. 39). Human beings may recognize injustice when they see it, yet remain completely blind for their contribution to injustice in the world. Subjects cannot recognize from within the interiority of inner-subjectivity their failure to live up to their own moral code. At a primordial level, living beings take themselves to be a totality, being ignorant of the exterior world' (pp. 30-34). The appearance of the 'first thought', therefore, is the moment of the birth of conscience, or of ethical awakening. See 'The Ego and Totality', in *Collected Philosophical Papers* (trans. Alphonso Lingis; Dordrecht, Netherlands: Martinus Hijhoff Publishers, 1987), pp. 25-48.

becomes the predicate to communion with the other made in the image of God, thus, affirming his/her irreplaceable intrinsic value that negates commodification and utilitarian reductionism. As humanity is reconnected to the One who is life itself (eternally and fully), the divine communal reality overtakes the complex tapestry of human inter-sociality, saturating, healing, and redeeming all until the life of God becomes the life of redeemed humanity – the perichoretic Trinitarian life in a human communal form.

In light of the above, it is impossible to think about redemption as a socially-disembodied personal experience. Instead, we should think of redemption as the process of bringing all social relationships that comprise our human identity within the presence of God – within the fellowship of the communal Trinity. Christ's Incarnation makes this redemption possible by birthing forth the embodied reality of the eternal Word of God as Scripture-in-relationships, as Scripture applied to the totality of human social existence. Thus, in the scandalous particularity of the Incarnation, Jesus the Christ (the Savior of the world) is born as a first-century Jew in Palestine under Roman occupation. He is someone's son and grandson, brother and cousin, teacher to his followers who are both male and female, young and old, slave and free, tax collectors and Roman soldiers, synagogue leaders and Pharisees, Jews and Gentiles, poor and rich. He heals their broken bodies and spirits, opens their eyes, illuminates their minds and hearts, and nurtures them with words of eternal life while multiplying on their behalf bread and fish, extending to them the fellowship of the social Trinity. This is an extension of the hospitality of God who has not quarantined Himself away from human life, but has taken it upon Himself, sanctifying and redeeming it in His own divine communal reality.

The radical socio-cultural particularity of the incarnation makes an explicit claim upon all aspects of human inter-sociality. The Word of God in flesh takes upon itself the nuanced ethnographic, geo-political, and economic distinctives of a particular culture in concrete geographical and temporal/historical location in order to authenticate the incarnation – the full extent of God's experience of authentic humanness, both in its particularity and universality. For He truly has to be the new/last Adam in whom access to the life of God as life eternal is restored to all of Adam's offspring. Thus, Christ takes upon Himself the particularity and universality of human culture in order to redeem all culture/s as an integral part of the human identity and experience.

Through the Incarnation, Christ brings the reality of human culture into the inner-life of God – the life of the Social Trinity. Yet, while humanity is the creation of God, culture is the creation of humanity[34] – it is the accumulative, transgenerational human project of world-making that manifests human creativity, evoking its origin in the infinite divine creative energy. Thus, in Christ, in a gesture of radical divine hospitality, God brings the human project of culture into Himself in order to redeem all that is human – the totality of what constitutes humanness. As the Greek Patristic tradition affirms in the words of St. Gregory of Nazianzus,

> For that which He [Christ] has not assumed He has not healed; but that which is united to His Godhead is also saved. If only half Adam fell, then that which Christ assumes and saves may be half also; but if the whole of his nature fell, it must be united to the whole nature of Him that was begotten, and so be saved as a whole.[35]

Thus, culture as human distinctive, redeemed and sanctified, becomes forever present in the Trinitarian communal life through the completeness of the Incarnation of the Son. For indeed, in the totality of the incarnation, nothing remains outside the reach of salvation, 'nothing can be taken away from the Son of man'.[36]

In the reality of the Incarnation, it is not surprising that the project of human civilization is brought into the project of God – Eden (as the primordial memory of the lost paradise) welcomes the

---

[34] We have come to define culture as 'what we make of the world'. See Andy Crouch, *Culture Making: Recovering Our Creative Calling* (Downer Grove, IL: IVP Books, 2008), p. 23. Therefore, while nature is the creation of God, culture is the creation of humanity. See also Tenner, *Theories of Culture*, pp. 28-29 and H. Richard Niebuhr, *Christ and Culture* (New York: Harper&Row Publishers, 1975), pp. 32-34. Niebuhr concludes that 'Culture is the "artificial, secondary environment" which man superimposes on the natural. It comprises language, habits, ideas, beliefs, customs, social organization, inherited artifacts, technical processes, and values' (p. 32). 'The world so far as it is man-made and man-intended is the world of culture' (p. 34).

[35] St. Gregory of Nazianzus, *Epistle CI. To Cledonius the Priest Against Apollinarius.*

[36] Alexander Schmemann, 'The Missionary Imperative', p. 201.

human city, for on its journey back to Eden, humanity has become impossible without it. The city, this iconic quintessentially human project (landmark of human civilization) that spatially condenses and compresses human sociality (bringing all diverse human relationships into a closer proximity to one another and thus, intensifying the social human identity) is brought into the infinite vastness of the inter-sociality of the Trinity. There it is faced with its ultimate transfiguring as the city of humanity becomes absorbed into God's vision of the world's future. Thus, God's future for the world acquires a new form – not a new Eden, but the New Jerusalem descends from heaven at the end of history as the polis of God becomes the polis of humanity (Revelation 21). The new order of the socio-political reality of the Kingdom does not advent into this world as a new garden but as a new polis. Apart from this eschatological openness and radical redemptive hospitality for human civilization, the comprehensive redemption of humanity will be impossible. As in the Incarnation, so in the final global advent of His Kingdom, God is not afraid that He would be contaminated by what is human. He takes upon Himself the totality of humanness in order to redeem it.

The Liturgical Transfiguring of Culture in the Christoformed Pentecost Community

The event of Pentecost displays the triumph of this redemption of cultural diversity within the singularity of Christ's Body on earth saturated by the Spirit. The languages of the world are brought together in the unity of the message. The singularity of the Word has applied itself to the multiplicity of cultures as their immediate purpose, pointing to their ultimate redemption in the Cosmic Christ. The Word, in return, takes upon itself the form and shape of the ethnic tongues – the iconic marker of ethnic diversity. Once again, God the Word is not afraid of being polluted by human culture, and as the Spirit conceives it in Christ's Body – the Church – as a living extension of His incarnated presence, the Word once again becomes flesh with all of the radical cultural particularity embraced by the first Incarnation. As in the Incarnation of the Son, the Spirit makes Christ's Body, the Church, a partaker in culture and, in return, the Church, by virtue of being a partaker of the divine nature brings human culture into the inner-life of the Communal Trinity. In the Incarnation of the Son, Jesus Christ embraces the totality of the human cultural experience still remaining without sin, so that all of it may be redeemed. In the same way, the Church as His incarnational presence in the world is given the mandate to participate in culture without partaking in its sins. Thus, being in the world, but not of the world, the Church is not afraid of being world-contaminated (Jn 17.13-19). She rises on the day of Pentecost as Christ's Body sent by the Lord into the world in the power of the Holy Spirit. The church enters culture as the countercultural reality of the Kingdom – the sociopolitical order and cultural substance of the redeemed human community. Yet, she takes culture upon herself, in order to sanctify and redeem it. This communal Body of Christ who has overcome sin, death, and the grave is to express collectively in Christ-likeness the totality of the human social experience, yet without sin.

In the life of the Church, culture becomes liturgy – the divine presence transforms the human project into means of grace, into a redemptive pedagogy of the divine communal life. Thus, art, architecture, poetry, music, rhetoric as 'a second creation'[37] that has found its origin and inspiration in 'the supreme art' of divine creativity (as described in the book of Genesis)[38] participates in the recreating of the world into the Kingdom of God. For, as H.A.H. Bartholomew points out, 'Beauty is a call, beyond the here and now, to the original principle and purpose of the world'.[39] It is a call to the ontological goodness and perfection of the material creation that reflects the beauty and goodness of the Creator and echoes the loving divine response to the breathtaking splendor of the world – it is good (Gen. 1.4, 12, 18, 21, 25, 30, 31). Yet, it is also a call to the eschatological transfiguring and summation of all in Christ – the purpose of salvific history. The redemptive teleology of beauty raptures the mind and the heart into the future of the world – the fusion of heaven and earth in Christ who makes all things new (Rev. 21.5). Creation (including the human body) is pregnant with urgent expectation of this renewal (Rom. 8.22-23) that starts with the In-

---

[37] St. Gregory of Nyssa, *Homily 11*, pp. 4-5.
[38] Bartholomew I, *Encountering the Mystery*, p. 23.
[39] Bartholomew I, *Encountering the Mystery*, p. 28.

carnation and the birth of the new humanity in the last Adam (1 Cor. 15.45) and ends with the new heaven and new earth (Rev. 21.1) that includes the new city – the New Jerusalem – the redeemed form of human culture (Rev. 21.2). Because both nature (the creation of God) and culture (the creation of humanity) are recapitulated in Christ, they are transfigured in the eschatological renewal and healing of the cosmos as He unites into Himself heaven and earth, the beginning and the end.

The church of Pentecost, herself a sacrament 'for the life of the world' (Jn 6.51) living in the 'ancient future' between the first and the second *parousia* of the Lamb, embodies, mediates, articulates, and enacts this process of cosmic renewal in her liturgical life. The redeemed and Christoformed human community called to consecrate the whole world, becomes the time-space continuum of culture's transfiguring amidst the tension of the already and not-yet reality of God's Kingdom. It displays culture in a transformative procession 'from glory to glory' (2 Cor. 3.18) between objective and subjective sanctification. It is objectively sanctified by virtue of the believers' location in Christ, yet, it is still in a process of subjective sanctification on its journey towards attaining the fullness of His likeness. Therefore, the sacramental life of the Church continually brings culture face to face with its need of cleansing and consecration. In it Christ continues to wash the feet of His community of disciples who walk daily in the mud of the world and they, who are His Body, extend that sanctifying grace sacramentally to one another. Christ in our fellow-believer washes our feet, while reminding us that we have already been washed in the blood of the Lamb. In the sacramental gestures of the faith community, the Church, being herself God's sacrament to the world for the sake of its ultimate consecration unto the Cosmic Christ, becomes the sacred space where culture is faced with its redemptive transfiguration into the Kingdom.

The church's liturgical anamnesis commits to the Spirit what is still being perfected in order for it to be enabled to articulate perfection. The Spirit makes human culture the medium of this articulation as the encounter with the divine mystery takes the ordinary and the mundane and transfigures it into an extraordinary experience of heaven on earth. Thus, the divine presence transforms music into an assent to the throne of God where the community of faith joins the angelic choirs in exultation and adoration of the Ancient of Days (Dan. 7.9). It unveils the icons and frescoes of the saints (the Church victorious) as windows to heaven and glimpses of 'the great cloud of witnesses' (Heb. 12.1) that surrounds us as we join the echo of their voices over the span of two millennia in proclamation of the core of our faith: 'We have seen the Resurrection of Christ'[40] and now He lives in us as we live in Him. The nearness of the Spirit turns bricks and mortar into a sanctuary, bread and wine into an eschatological feast/banquet, inspired speech into spiritual food, and the community of faith into a living embodied extension of the Resurrected Savior on earth. The Spirit takes what is and makes it what is to come before the spiritual eyes of the beholder who sees the advent of the *eschata* in the midst of the present until the now is transfigured in its future form. Thus, the epiclesis of the divine presence is a conditioning for a new way of seeing the world – a new worldview as an outcome of liturgical (trans-) formation.[41] Our vision of the world emerges through the lenses of the vision of God. We see the world bathed in the brilliant light of Mt. Tabor's transfigured and transfiguring Christ – we see it as a gift of grace, beauty and goodness that reflects the glory of God. Such a vision mandates a different way of relating to the world – not as to a disposable commodity but as to a sacrament of social transformation into the likeness of God. Such a vision makes the life of the Trinity 'the social program' of humanity.[42] As H.A.H. Bartholomew states,

> Every form of community – the work-place, the school, the city, even a nation – has as its vocation to become, each in its own way, a living icon of the Trinity. Nations are called to be transparent to one another, just as the three persons of the Trinity are transparent to one another. Such is surely part of the role of religion in a changing world – namely, to promote freedom among human beings as the basis of encounter and communion.[43]

---

[40] An ancient Christian chant that is still proclaimed in Orthodox liturgy during every service of matins and for forty days after Easter (Bartholomew I, *Encountering the Mystery*, p. 35).

[41] For a great articulation of the dialectic of the movement from worship/liturgy to worldview see Smith, *Desiring the Kingdom*, pp. 133-54.

[42] Bartholomew I, *Encountering the Mystery*, p. 133.

[43] Bartholomew I, *Encountering the Mystery*, p. 133.

The City of God as the Eschatological Vision of Redeemed Culture

Pentecost's polyglotic summoning of all nations under heaven by the proclamation of the Good News of God in their ethnic tongue is an in-breaking of the *eschata* and a prophetic foretaste of all ethnicities' joined destiny in Christ. We catch a glimpse of this glorious *telos* in the magnificent vision of redeemed humanity articulated in the book of Revelation. The vision crescendos into a breathtaking narrative of the worshiping multitude 'standing before the throne' of God and the Lamb (Rev. 7.9).[44] This colossal human mass that no eye can count moves in sacramental singularity of purpose and desire, worshiping its Redeemer, washed in His blood, sanctified by His Spirit. Yet, here John sees represented every tongue and every nation of the world. They are distinctly identifiable; they have not lost their ethnographic uniqueness in that redeemed oneness. Their white robes point to the common experience of redemption and sanctification. The multitude is one with the Savior. Yet, they stand before God not only as Christ's one Body but also as persons, nations and cultures, for He has preserved diversity within oneness.

The culmination of the redemption of human culture is introduced to us with the image of the New Jerusalem descending from the new heaven to the new earth (Revelation 21). Its arrival is an-

---

[44] For an expanded exposition on Rev. 7.9 see Thomas, *The Apocalypse: A Literary and Theological Commentary*. I am also deeply indebted to Professor Thomas' insights in highlighting the symbolic meanings of the complex depiction of the City of God in Revelation 21. In his notes on Revelation 7, Thomas discusses the contrast between the group of the 144,000 who are numbered and this multitude that no one is able to number. According to Thomas, 'The sheer magnitude of this innumerable crowd could not help but be an extraordinary encouragement to them [John's audience] as they face what at that point must seem to be insurmountable odds' (p. 467). Further, while the 144,000 are from each of the tribes of Israel, this crowd is composed out of all nations and tribes and peoples and tongues. The white robes indicate that this crowd has proven faithful to the witness of Jesus and reminds the reader of the white robes 'given to the souls under the altar that have been slaughtered "on account of the Word of God and the witness which they had"' (p. 269). The palm branches remind the reader of Jesus' triumphal entry in Jerusalem (Jn 12.13). The cry of the crowd is 'Salvation to our God who sits on the throne and to the Lamb'. Thomas comments that, 'This hymn-like confession conveys a sense of finality, as it appears to focus upon salvation in its most comprehensive, eschatological sense as belonging to "our God Who Sits on the throne and the Lamb"' (p. 269).

nounced by the angelic herald as the advent of the Bride of the Lamb – the trans-epochal community of saints transfigured into the likeness of God. Indeed, this is the Church in her *theosis*.[45] Thus, the future of God for humanity manifested in the descent of 'heaven on earth' arrives in the form of a city. The distinctly human cultural project has been transfigured into a sacred space for it has become the temple of God on earth. The City of God has become the city of humanity so that the city of humanity may become God's temple. This is human culture in its redeemed form. The revelation that the city is His temple (a Holy of Holies as indicated by its cubic form) is articulated by the text starting the numbering of the city gates with the ones facing East – a depiction evoking the temple in Jerusalem (Rev. 21.13).[46] Yet, in contrast to the old Jerusalem temple, all humanity is given radically inclusive access to the sanctuary that is the City of God (vv. 24-27). The nations come into it from all corners of the world – even from these parts that had previously opposed God.[47] The kings of the earth bring the glories of the nations into the New Jerusalem. The accomplishments and splendor of human civilization are presented as offerings into this temple, into the Holy of Holies that is the City of God. They are redemptively incorporated into the new life of the city – life as a continual liturgy that unites heaven and earth in worship of the One and Only God. Here all human creativity and cultural achievements, all value and beauty stand reunited with their divine origin and *telos*. What humanity has treasured, pursued, and desired has been reevaluated and reordered in this offering to God, as human affections have been realigned with Kingdom life and Christoformed into love towards God and neighbor. Now, humanity is free to love and be loved rightly, and therefore to worship truly in that very worship that transforms it into the likeness of God.

The names of the twelve tribes of Israel (the seed of Abraham) are inscribed on the city gates (Rev. 21.12), yet their precise order and location remains unknown to the reader. Perhaps there are two

---

45 See the section on 'The City of God' in Chapter 2 of the present book.

46 Thomas, *The Apocalypse*, p. 646.

47 Regarding the text's implication for the conversion of the former enemies of God – the once upon a time rebellious nations who now are depicted as beneficiaries of the redeeming grace of God – see Thomas, *The Apocalypse*, pp. 640-41 and 654-56.

immediate levels of implication of this omission of information. On the one hand, the order of inscription is irrelevant, because all nations enter through these gates, for all nations are to be blessed in Abraham's seed (Gen. 18.18). On the other hand, all those who enter the city that is the bride of Christ become seed of Abraham, the father of faith (Rom. 4.16). As Thomas indicates, twelve becomes a number of perfection, pointing to the completion of God's perfect plan for humanity.[48] This thought is further magnified in the display of the foundations of the city walls that are inscribed with the names of the twelve apostles (v. 14). The implication of this revelation points to the foundational witness of the apostles of Christ in relation to the building of His Church – His bride – the community of the saints. That very witness has been taken to the uttermost parts of the world through the command to make disciples of all nations (Mt. 28.19). Now the nations, in response to this witness, have entered the city from the four corners of the world and have been transformed by the Spirit into the city's very substance – they have become part of that city on a hill that radiates forth the glory of God. The gospel has been preached to the uttermost parts of the earth transfiguring it into the City of God that now has covered the globe (v. 17). This global megalopolis has united heaven and earth, God and humanity, as the redeemed human community has become God's sanctuary on earth.

In view of the fact that the entire city is a temple – a sacred space of worship to God where the worshipers have become truly and completely one with Him – the description of the holy city culminates with the observation that there is no temple in it (Rev. 21.22). The Lord God, the Almighty, and the Lamb are its temple. Here once again the fusion of the city with the Holy of Holies and the saints comes into view. The believers have been the temple of God on earth (1 Cor. 3.16); now they are the very living stones/fibers of the heavenly city where God is the temple. God has become one with His people; Christ has become all in all. As Thomas remarks,

> The relationship between God and his people in the holy city Jerusalem represents complete integration of God with his people,

---

[48] Thomas, *The Apocalypse*, p. 639.

with the mention of the Lamb underscoring the means by which salvation is accomplished.[49]

No doubt, this is a glimpse of humanity's new reality of being. The transformative dialectic of the Spirit reveals the Church before the eyes of the beholder in her eternal form, yet her breathtaking beauty and glow are somehow endearingly close and familiar. The familiarity and the enchantment with the non-articulable otherness of the *novum* blend in an inner certainty of homecoming until the viewer grasps the truth – in the mystery of salvation, the Church has always been precisely what she is in her glorious eschatological fulfillment – the place where God dwells, the place where He has built a home for all His creatures. Therefore, in the ecstatic wonder of the never-seen-before, somehow it is not surprising to see that humanity is indwelled by God and transformed into His temple on earth through the agency of the Holy Spirit, nor that humanity indwells God and partakes in the divine nature. Yet, there is a sense of articulation of a new level of reality of complete and total union of the creature with the Creator. Now humanity has truly become one with God – it has attained *theosis*. As prophesied by Isaiah (60.19-20), 'the glory of God has illuminated' the city and 'his lamp is the Lamb' (Rev. 21.23).[50] Christ, the light of the world, has transformed His Body – the Church – into the light of the new heaven and the new Earth. She, the bride, shines with His radiance, illuminating all existence. Yet, since the beginning, this has been her very mission in the world – shining in the darkness the glory of the Lamb, making the invisible God visible in the Body of the Son. She has been given the light that the world could not overtake (Jn 1.5) and now stands as the world's radiant future, making once again Christ present as its very light.

---

[49] Thomas, *The Apocalypse*, p. 653. See also R. Hollis Gause, *Revelation: God's Stamp of Sovereignty on History* (Cleveland, TN: Pathway Press, 1983), p. 273. Gause highlights v. 22 as 'the fulfillment of the tabernacling of God among His redeemed people' and 'the fulfillment of the four-square nature of the city'. As Gause states, 'John is here saying that this entire city is the sanctuary of God. There is no Temple, but God is the fulfillment of the Temple … The presence of God and His redeeming Lamb constitute the Temple; this is the realm of glory, and it is immediate to all in the city.'

[50] Thomas, *The Apocalypse*, p. 653.

In this luminous redeemed form, culture is reunited with nature – the creation of humanity welcomes the creation of God as humanity enters heaven on earth. Humanity is finally at home – it is in paradise. The very essence of recovered Eden in the life of the paradisiacal city is revealed through the vision of

> … a river of living water clear as crystal, coming out of the throne of God and of the Lamb in the middle of its street. And on either side of the river was the tree of life, bearing twelve kinds of fruit yielding its fruit every month; and the leaves of the tree were for the healing of the nations (Rev. 22.1-2).[51]

Unhindered access to life and healing for all humanity – this is, indeed, a restored entry into Eden within the divine architecture of the city. There the seed of the first Adam that has now become the communal form of the last Adam is given (in Him) renewed access to the tree of life, being welcomed beyond the boundaries of time into eternity. The vision reminds the human creature of its dependence on God even on the other side of time. For, indeed, all that is created has a beginning and therefore is contingent upon the One Who alone is without beginning or an end. Thus, eternity is given as a gift of divine hospitality to the new humanity in the form of unlimited access to unceasing sustenance and wholeness that proceeds from the very presence of God and is available to all who have become one with Him.

The restoration of humanity to Eden is sealed by the long anticipated announcement that there is no longer any curse, that 'the throne of God and the Lamb' (Rev. 22.3) is there, and 'they shall see His face, and His name shall be on their foreheads' (v. 4). The lifting of the curse is the erasing of the consequences of the fall for creation. This includes ending the enmity between human beings competing against one another for access to life, as well as between the anthropic and the non-anthropic creation (the latter resisting its

---

[51] Gause points out that Rev. 22.1-2 describes 'the eternal fulfillment of the predictions of Ezekiel' (Ezek. 47.1-11) (*Revelation*, p. 275). The living water that flows from the very presence of God in the middle of the street of the city and the tree of life that lines its banks both 'provide the benefits of the atonement' to all of the city's urban dwellers (p. 276). A natural outcome of this comprehensive application of 'the atonement provision and application' is that the curse is eliminated – 'None of the blight of sin exists any longer' (p. 276).

violent commodification, exploitation, and extinction induced by human greed and self-indulgence). The end of the curse means peace between humanity and nature and the reunion of all of God's creation in the gift of paradise.[52] There humanity sees God once again face to face and is imprinted with His name as His own possession – a mark of belonging and protection. God is enthroned in the midst of His people – the breathtaking luminous city – for His will is being now done on earth as it is in heaven (Mt. 6.10), apprehending in the divine life both nature and culture. The prayer of Christ that has been at the heart of the intercession of the Church on behalf of the world has been granted. Heaven and earth have been fused into oneness within the redeemed form of global humanity – the form of Christ who has recapitulated the cosmos into himself and made all things new.

---

52 For an expanded articulation of the way God's providence moves both humanity and the rest of creation towards its eschatological renewal in Christ see Dimitru Staniloae, *The World: Creation and Deification*, pp. 205-15.

EPILOGUE: SOME THOUGHTS FOR FURTHER EXPLORATION

The Event of Pentecost as a Paradigm for Social Transformation

As the resurrection of the Son of Man seals the victory over death, it induces the eschatological expectation of the ultimate goal of the world's redemptive transfiguration, namely the renewal of all things in the Cosmic Christ.[1] The resurrection asserts the assurance of the inevitability of cosmic justice at the second coming of the Lord, whose journey has already begun from beyond the ends of the historical horizon.[2] "'I am the Alpha and the Omega", says the Lord God, "who is and who was and who is coming, the Almighty'" (Rev. 1.8). These are words of hope for the ones who have been caged in the grasp of empires and forbidden to dream of an alternative socio-political future for the world. This is the liberation manifesto of human imagination, the foundation of dissident resistance against the dehumanizing social deformities induced and perpetuated by imperial coercion. It is the divine proclamation that all earthly empires shall come to an end and their projects for self-immortalization will fail in the face of the earthly advent of God's Kingdom that is not of this world (Jn 18.36). The Kingdom of Heaven looms beyond the historical horizon as the great destabi-

---

[1] On the significance of resurrection see also Oliver O'Donovan, *Resurrection and Moral Order: An Outline for Evangelical Ethics* (Grand Rapids, MI: Eerdmans, 1994), pp. 13, 57.

[2] The present participle that is translated in English 'the one who is coming' could be viewed as an indicative of an implicit action that has been already initiated and is currently unfolding.

lizer of imperial political expediency. It offers the lenses through which we see the present age's empires for what they truly are, unmasking[3] their propaganda disguise. The Kingdom brings to light the impotence of imperial promises for social salvation and unveils the self-serving teleology of their political agendas. It is an empowering tool of restored vision and grasp of the very Truth that sets the captives free (Jn 8.32) – the Truth that is Christ Himself, the *pantokrator* and redeemer of all.

The vision of the Kingdom provides the mechanisms of discerning the difference between the truth that births the fruit of God's future for the world and the deceptive promises of attaining the content of heaven on earth through alternative socio-political means. It teaches the one who has eyes to see the simple logic of redemption undergirding the historical process as understood through the revelation of the age to come: what we see in the present that we do not see in the vision of the Kingdom has no future – it shall come to an end. The Spirit who moves history towards the *eschaton* gifts this illuminating vision (as an enduring banner of hope and assurance that no injustice shall inherit the Kingdom) to the ones whose cries for justice are silenced by the present age. The Spirit births forth the community of faith as the Kingdom's historically-contextualized embodiment and a tangible evidence of eschatological inevitability. He unveils before the eyes of the world the vision of the coming Christ that pierces history with the expectation of bringing to an end all things that have distorted God's creation and have exhausted the world by making it an end in itself.[4] The incarnation has recapitulated the world into Christ so that His death and resurrection may restore it to wholeness. In Him the world stands healed and renewed. What has devoured and exhausted the world is now itself exhausted in the Cosmic Christ. Thus, the violent commodification of creation that reduces it to mere means of self-indulgence through greedy, gluttonous consumption (of things and beings) for one's own benefit (with no concern for the well-

---

[3] See Smith, *Desiring the Kingdom*, p. 92. Smith discusses apocalyptic literature as 'a genre of Scripture that tries to get us to see (or see through) the empires that constitute our environment, in order to see them for what they really are ... the point of apocalyptic literature is not predicting but unmasking'.

[4] Schmemann, *For the Life of the World*, p. 16.

being of the other) has no future – it is not the final word of history. Christ is coming to become all in all (Eph. 1.21). This marvelous Christoforming transfiguration of the world starts with the Church as the Body of Christ, the household of God until, through His Body, the entire world becomes a church – a sanctuary for all of God's creatures.

The event of Pentecost marks the beginning of this Spirit-conceived transfiguration of the world. It authenticates this eschatological hope and its transformational power and seals the incarnation of the socio-political reality of the Kingdom within the Church, raising her as a living extension of the resurrected and resurrecting Christ. Thus, the Church of Pentecost, conceived and empowered by the Spirit of the end, presents the ecumenical eschatological future of the world. The remainder of this epilogue highlights some further reflections on the theological foundations undergirding the socio-transformative dimensions of Pentecost, which deserve additional exploration beyond the scope of the present book.

Pentecost as a Contextual Necessity within the Global Village

It takes a Pentecost to empower the Church for her mission and reconstitute her socio-political relevance in the polyphonic context of the contemporary global village. In the striking multicultural diversity of globalized human existence, the Church needs Pentecost in order to be able to articulate life-transforming truth in the multiplicity of tongues of the village's residents while maintaining the integrity of the message.

The biblical account of first-century Jerusalem on the day of Pentecost displays a certain symbolic association with today's cosmopolitan life in the world's urban centers. In their spatially condensed existence, representatives of 'all nations under heaven' are gathered together within one another's reach in the close proximity outlined by the boundaries of the human city (Acts 2.5). The empowerment of the Church (the redeemed human community) through the decent of the Holy Spirit created an event in ancient Jerusalem that captivated the attention of its dwellers. It disturbed the ordinary city life staging a divinely-ordained moment of encounter with a new socio-political reality on earth – the advent of

God's Kingdom within the human community. The conception of the Kingdom in the Body of Christ was announced by image ('tongues of fire') and sound ('like of a violent, rushing wind') in the theophany of the Spirit. The resonance and the vibrations of the event drew the crowds as the gospel reached each one present 'in his/her own language' (Acts 2.6-11). The event transcended the ruptures within the human communal tapestry bringing about euphonic oneness in the polyphony of sustained multicultural diversity. Its tangible outcome was a healed human community that erased the post-Babel fractures of human sociality. Pentecost brought about a new communal ontology in which fear and suspicion towards the stranger, conflict and competition with the other were eradicated by the Spirit's translation and embodiment of the divine communal life within the new human *socium* of the redeemed. The convergence of human languages was an audible manifestation of this new way of being with the other that brings to an end the silencing, negation, and dismissal of their voice. It opened the eyes of the ones who embraced the message of Pentecost to see the image of God in the strangeness of the other and to recognize him/her as belonging to the same family. What Babel had obscured as being strange and foreign, Pentecost revealed as being once again close and familiar – it transfigured the other before the very eyes of the faith community into a brother and a sister within the household of the Father.

In the urban estrangement of a world terrorized by a claustrophobic fear of strangers and violently threatened by inter-cultural conflicts with the ethnic and religious other, the human city is desperate for Pentecost. It is desperate for the Spirit's transfiguring work that births forth the new human community of mutual understanding, acceptance and love towards one's neighbor – a community living out the divine hospitality that heals a fractured world.

Further, in contrast to the fragmenting spirits of this age, Pentecost's vision of creation's renewal joins in eschatological oneness 'all flesh' (Acts 2.17) through the *kenosis* of the Spirit. This is an act of radical emancipation and equalization of significance of all forms and locations of life, while affirming and preserving their diversity and uniqueness. It deconstructs the notion of power-mapping the world by fragmenting it into centers and margins, and dissolves social stigmas and apologetics of stratification and exclusion.

In light of that, the event of Pentecost provides a paradigm for the Church's incarnation of a transculturally relevant process of authentic social transformation towards universal human emancipation in the life of a Spirit-saturated global community. Therefore, the accomplishment of the mission of the Church and the articulation of its message demands the empowerment of Pentecost (Acts 1.8). The experience of Pentecost could be seen as a contextual necessity in the contemporary global village that primes with the life of the Spirit the human community (traumatized by tribalism and religious conflicts) towards multicultural harmony and social redemption. The Spirit becomes the immediate environment in which foreign tongues make sense and intercultural human understanding becomes once again possible as God anoints the heralds and the hearers of the message. Thus, Pentecost highlights the presence of the Spirit as a necessity also for establishing and articulating what constitutes the Good News for today – a message that transcends ethnocentric political agendas guiding the diverse multitude towards a common vision of human flourishing in the global polis.

Pentecost as a Necessity in Articulating what Constitutes the Good News for Today

Pentecost is the trans-epochal vehicle of translating the life of God (of the Trinitarian proto-community) into the realities of human communal existence and, thus, of seeding the world's future (the Kingdom of God) into the present. The missiological genius of its incarnational medium highlights the radical hospitality of God whose grace comes to us by taking the form of our need and absorbing it redemptively into the divine life in order to meet it fully and perfectly. Thus, the news of the approaching Kingdom arrives as a tangibly en-fleshed gospel that addresses contextually critical human needs within the present and generates a transformative hope that fuels the socio-political imagination towards re-envisioning of the world's future.

The Church, as a harvest of the gospel, is herself an embodied gospel – a good news for the world. In the gospel the human words are transformed into the Word of God and in a manifestation of the Kingdom.[5] As the very Word of God, the gospel is *theophorus* (God-bearing), and so is also the fruit of the Spirit in the life of the Church. In them 'the eternal coming'[6] of the Risen Lord to His own marks the Body of Christ as the unique location of those who see His coming and recognize His tangible healing presence on earth in their very midst. This is the Church's life as God's sacrament to the world in the ancient-future between the first and the second *parousia*.

What the public hears broadcasted as the good news on the day of Pentecost is the narrative of the life of God pro-actively intervening on behalf of humanity in the midst of its current existential struggles. The crowds are, therefore, compelled to ask the question 'What does this mean?' (Acts 2.12) The answer starts with pointing to their location in time (one of the most precious coordinates for the time-compressed human existence) by positioning them at the unfolding of the *eschata* (Acts 2.17). Further, a vision of the future of the world is offered – a vision of striking democratization, of radical emancipation, and inclusivity permeating all social strata across gender, age, economic, and socio-political differences (Acts 2.17-18). As the third Person of the Trinity pours Himself upon 'all flesh', God invites all of humanity to partake in His life as in the very future of the world destined for transfiguration into the likeness of God. The vision indicates a journey (a process of discovery, adventure, and possible perils). Yet, simultaneously, it constitutes a promise for arrival, for it is a visitation from the future, which is as inevitable as the very God who inhabits its fulfillment. The Spirit articulates this vision as celebration of diversity in unity through the gift of articulating one's experience of personal transformation (in and with God) in the language of the other and the different, embracing them as part of the future in an act of worship 'in Spirit and Truth' (Jn 4.23).

The Church (the 120 from the Upper Room enlarged to 3,120 by the end of the proclamation) authenticates the message through her experience. She stands before the crowds as the embodiment of the very future of the world (Acts 2.43-47) – the Body of the Resurrected Christ, the ultimate purpose of all existence, the infinite di-

---

[5] Schmemann, *For the Life of the World*, p. 33.
[6] Schmemann, *For the Life of the World*, p. 33.

vine presence (Mt. 28.20, Heb. 13.5) that makes eternity tangible within the inter-sociality of the faith community. Therefore, the prophetic voice of the Church in the power of the Spirit is authenticated by Christ's Messianic reign in her midst as the future of justice and peace abiding in the present. The heavenly Jerusalem descends on earth in the earthly Jerusalem through the life of the Church – the life of God in a human communal form. The good news is that heaven on earth as a loving community, as Sabbath and Shalom, as comprehensive justice and access to life for all of God's creatures could be experienced here and now in the household of God though humanity's Christoforming ontological renewal. The transformation of the world is the dialectical outcome of this redemptive transfiguration of the human community in the likeness of the Triune God. This is an illuminated perspective on the possibility of a hopeful social transformation as healing of human communal existence and the rest of creation that starts with the ontological renewal of each separate individual. Yet, conversely, it takes a Christoformed community to heal each individual human life through its loving inclusion into the life of the Triune God as an expression of the divine communal hospitality. This understanding magnifies the moral responsibility to see the other through the eyes of God and love them with His love, allowing the divine nature to heal our own distorted vision and understanding of the other, blurred and tainted by prejudice, hatred and competition for access to life.

Pentecost as a Necessity for the Future of the Church

As Pentecost empowers the Church to be the world's future within the present, it challenges the faith community towards its own continual transfiguration from glory to glory (2 Cor. 3.18). In so doing, Pentecost establishes an ethical demand for all-inclusive emancipation, not on the basis of evolutionary wisdom and survival reflex, but as the claim of the future upon the present. The Spirit inspires the voices of the sons and daughters (Acts 2.17) whose prophetic utterance is mediated not only through the content of the message, but also by virtue of the incarnated future of the Church. To negate their voices is to deny one's future. The voices of the children become the voice of God who calls the Church to embrace the metamorphic work of the Spirit towards its ultimate form and character. This transfiguration involves accepting the discomfort of abandoning one's form and content for another – that of the future, of the age to come. Therefore, Pentecost invites a multigenerational fusion within the communal image of Christ – the future form of the Church. Christ's Body, endowed with Pentecost power becomes a bridge of overcoming transgenerational tensions and conflicts into the healing embrace of the Spirit. Then young people can see visions (a quality usually associated with spiritual maturity, as well as with appeased passions, soberness, and objectivity that may come with experience and age); and old people can dream dreams (a quality associated with the passionate pursuits of the youth and their imaginative engagement of the world). The youth's clarity of vision and the elders' passion for life display a new and otherworldly form of generational fusion – a form of reconciliation between the present and the future if wholesome oneness and commitment to God's world-transfiguring work. Therefore, it takes Pentecost to heal transgenerational ruptures, tensions, and misunderstandings while empowering the voice of the children and giving to the elders ears to hear and eyes to see the message of the Spirit in their lives. Pentecost demands commitment to the future that God has gifted and incarnated to the Church, teaching the community of faith to be a good steward of its tangible presence in the life of the children.

Furthermore, the Spirit-empowered voices not only of the sons but also of the daughters penetrate the Church with prophetic urgency. As God chooses to speak with a female voice, He shakes and shifts the ecclesial Body through the content of the Kingdom, dissecting and separating the transient from the eternal (Heb. 4.12) and the human-made from the divine. Thus, in Pentecost the eternal Body of Christ visits the present addressing it through the voices of its prophesying daughters, while confirming their radical counter-cultural identity as coming in the now from the very future of the Church. As such, they stand out in the life of the faith community as prophetic road signs and pointers to that future. The peculiar persistence of the Spirit in anointing the daughters for the task of ministry in the face of culturally-preconditioned and institutionally-endorsed gender-exclusion points to Pentecost as offering a continual pedagogy on discerning God's voice in the female voices of the faith community. It opens the believers' eyes to see through the partitions of cultural prejudices how the invisible Spirit chooses to make himself visible by clothing God's daughters with the divine presence that rests upon them unashamed of and undisturbed by their female bodies. God is unapologetic in His choice to indwell them and make them His heralds and sanctuary on earth. He is not afraid of being contaminated by them. After all, they are His creation – wonderfully and fearfully made in the breathtaking beauty of God's own likeness.

Conclusion: The Necessity of Pentecost as a Guarantee for Transformational Continuity between the Present and the Future

In contrast to many religious and secular visions of radical social discontinuity between this age and the age to come, in Pentecost the future of the world arrives into the 'now' for the sake of its redemptive transfiguring. This is an act of summoning the world face to face with its destiny and calling it on a journey of healing and renewal. Pentecost's prophetic edge does not manifest itself as an act of condemnation and withdrawal from the present in a desensitized bliss of eschatological escapism, nor of a violent, revolutionary negation of its substance. Instead, the Spirit conceives the future into the present, nurtures it, and cultivates it until this world is shaped into the age to come.

This vision of Pentecost illuminates our understanding that the future is impossible without the (gender, race, age, religion, and ethnic) other. Their presence is lifted up as a central element of the Christoforming pedagogy of the Spirit. Indeed, as Christ is formed in us we are capable to discern Him in the other. Christ, our future, meets us in the other's face as a reminder that our journey in God is ecumenical for it encompasses all of the *oikoumene* – we cannot arrive to the final destination without the other; if we are to have a future, we have to reach it together. As we learn to live together in the organic oneness of Christ's Body, we are united to God's communal life extending its hospitality to the rest of the world on the way to its final transfiguring into the divine likeness. This is the end of history – the global village becoming the city of God in the beauty and splendor of the Triune life. This is the beginning of eternity in humanity's Christoformed union with God.

Bibliography

Archer, Kenneth, 'Nourishment for Our Journey: The Pentecostal *Via Salutis* and Sacramental Ordinances', *Journal of Pentecostal Theology* 13.1 (2004), pp. 79-96.

Augustine, Daniela C., 'Pentecost as the Church's Cosmopolitan Vision of Civil Society', in William Storrar, Peter Casarella, and Paul Metzger (eds.), *A World for All? Global Civil Society in Political Theory and Trinitarian Theology* (Grand Rapids, MI: Eerdmans, 2011), pp. 197-220.

—'Pentecost and Prosperity in Eastern Europe: between Sharing of Possessions and Accumulating of Personal Wealth', in Katherine Attanasi and Amos Yong (eds.), *Pentecostalism and Prosperity: The Socio-Economics of the Global Charismatic Movements* (New York: Palgrave Macmillan, 2012), pp. 189-212.

Augustine, Saint, *City of God* (trans. G.G. Walsh, D.B. Zema, G. Monahan, and D.J. Honnan; New York: Doubleday, 1958).

Avinery, Shlomo, *Hegel's Theory of the Modern State* (Cambridge: Cambridge University Press, 1972).

Bakhtin, Mikhail, 'Discourse in the Novel', in Michael Holquist (ed.), *The Dialogic Imagination* (Austin, TX: The University of Texas Press, 1981).

—'Response to a Question from Novy Mir Editorial Staff,' in Caryl Emerson and Michael Holquist (eds.), *Speech Genres and Other Late Essays* (trans. Vern W. McGee; Austin, TX: The University of Texas, 1986), pp. 1-7.

Basil the Great, Saint, *On the Holy Spirit* (Crestwood, NY: St. Vladimir's Seminary Press, 1980).

Berberoglu, Beruch, *Globalization of Capital and the Nation-State: Imperialism, Class Struggle, and the State in the Age of Global Capitalism* (Lanham, MD: Rowman & Littlefield Publishers, 2003).

—(ed.), *Globalization and Change: The Transformation of Global Capital* (Lanham, MD: Lexington Books, 2005).

Berdyaev, Nikolas, *Philosophy of Inequality* (Sofia: Prozoretz, 1923).

—О Робстве и Свободе Человека (Paris: YMCA - Press, 1939).

—*The New Middle Ages*, vol. 2 of *Collected Works* (Sofia: Zachari Stoyanov, 2003).

—*The Meaning of History*, vol. 2 of *Collected Works* (Sofia: Zachari Stoyanov, 2003).

Birch, Kean and Vlad Mykhnenko, 'Introduction: A World Turned Right Way Up', in Kean Birch and Vlad Mykhnenko (eds.), *The Rise and Fall of Neoliberalism: The Collapse of an Economic Order* (New York: Zed Books, 2010), pp. 1-20.

Blanchard, Kathryn D., *The Protestant Ethic or the Spirit of Capitalism: Christians, Freedom, and Free Markets* (Eugene, OR: Cascade Books, 2010).

Blount, Brian K., 'The Apocalypse of Worship: A House of Prayer for all Nations', in Brian K. Blount and Leonora Tubbs Tisdale (eds.), *Making Room at the Table: An Invitation to Multicultural Worship* (Louisville, KY: Westminster John Knox Press, 2001), pp. 16-29.

Bruce, F.F., *Commentary on the Book of Acts* (The New International Commentary on the New Testament; ed. F.F. Bruce; Grand Rapids, MI: Eerdmans, 1979).

Brueggemann, Walter, *The Prophetic Imagination* (Minneapolis, MN: Fortress Press, 1978).

Bulgakov, Sergius, 'The Virgin and the Saints in Orthodoxy', in Daniel B. Clendenin (ed.), *Eastern Orthodox Theology: A Contemporary Reader* (Grand Rapids, MI: Baker Books, 1995), pp. 65-75.

Callinicos, Alex, *An Anti-Capitalist Manifesto* (Cambridge: Polity Press, 2003).

Calvin, John, *Institutes of the Christian Religion* (trans. Ford Lewis Battles; ed. John T. McNeil; Philadelphia: Westminster, 1960).

Cavanaugh, William T., *Being Consumed: Economics and Christian Desire* (Grand Rapids, MI: Eerdmans, 2008).

Crouch, Andy, *Culture Making: Recovering Our Creative Calling* (Downer Grove, IL: IVP Books, 2008).

Crossan, John Dominic, *God and Empire: Jesus Against Rome, Then and Now* (New York: Harper One, 2007).

Derrida, Jacques, *Adieu to Emmanuel Levinas* (Stanford, CA: Stanford University Press, 1990).

—*Given Time: I. Counterfeit Money* (trans. Peggy Kamuf; Chicago: University of Chicago Press, 1991).

—'The Force of Law: 'The Mystical Foundation of Authority', in Drucilla Cornell *et al.* (eds.), *Deconstruction and the Possibility of Justice*, (trans. Mary Quaintance; New York: Routledge, 1992), pp. pp. 68-91.

—*The Gift of Death* (trans. David Wills; Chicago: University of Chicago Press, 1995).

—*Deconstruction in a Nutshell: A Conversation with Jacques Derrida* (ed. John D. Caputo; New York: Fordham University Press, 1997).

—*Of Hospitality* (with parallel text by Anne Dufourmantelle; Stanford, CA: Stanford University Press, 2000).

—*On Cosmopolitanism and Forgiveness* (London: Routledge, 2001).

Dulles, Avery, *The Catholicity of the Church* (Oxford: Oxford University Press, 1987).

Elshtain, Jean Bethke, 'Democracy on Trial', in Don E. Eberly (ed.), *The Essential Civil Society Reader: Classic Essays in the American Civil Society Debate* (New York: Rowman & Littlefield Publishers, 2000), pp. 101-22.

Fernandez, Eleasar S., 'From Babel to Pentecost: Finding a Home in the Belly of Empire,' *Semeia* 90/91 (Spring-Summer 2002), pp. 29-51.

Finger, Reta Halterman, *Of Widows and of Meals: Communal Meals in the Book of Acts* (Grand Rapids, MI: W.B. Eerdmans, 2007).

Fukuyama, Francis, *The End of History and the Last Man* (New York: The Free Press, 1992).

Gause, R. Hollis, *Revelation: God's Stamp of Sovereignty on History* (Cleveland, TN: Pathway Press, 1983).

Gaventa, Beverly Roberts, *The Acts of the Apostles* (Abingdon New Testament Commentaries; Nashville, TN: Abingdon Press, 2003).

Green, Robert W. (ed.), *Protestantism and Capitalism: The Weber Thesis and Its Critics* (Boston: D.C. Heath and Company, 1959).

Goldingay, John, *Israel's Gospel* (Old Testament Theology, 1; Downers Grove, IL: InterVarsity Press, 2003).

Gorringe, Timothy, 'The Principalities and Powers: A Framework for Thinking about Globalization', in Peter Heslam (ed.) *Globalization and the Good* (London: SPCK, 2004), pp. 79-91.

Gordon Graham, *The Case Against the Democratic State* (Charlottesville, VA: Imprint Academics, 2002).

Gregory of Nazianzus, Saint, *The Fifth Theological Oration. On the Holy Spirit*, XXVI, in Cyril of Jerusalem and Gregory of Nazianzen, *Christian Classics Ethereal Library* (http://www.ccel.org/ccel/schaff/npnf 207.iii. xvii.html).

—St. Gregory of Nazianzus, *Epistle CI. To Cledonius the Priest Against Apollinarius.*

Groody, Daniel G., 'Globalizing Solidarity: Christian Anthropology and the Challenge of Human Liberation', *Theological Studies* 69 (2008), pp. 250-68.

Guroian, Vigen, 'Fruits of Pentecost: The Christian Gardener,' *The Christian Century*, 113.21 (July 3, 1996), pp. 684-86.

H.A.H. Bartholomew I, Archbishop of Constantinople and Ecumenical Patriarch, *Encountering the Mystery* (New York: Doubleday, 2008).

Hamilton, Victor P., *The Book of Genesis: Chapters 18-50* (Grand Rapids, MI: Eerdmans, 1995).

Hardt, Michael and Antonio Negri, *Empire* (Cambridge, MA: Harvard University Press, 2000).

—*Multitude: War and Democracy in the Age of Empire* (London: Penguin Books, 2005).

Harvey, David, *A Brief History of Neoliberalism* (New York: Oxford University Press, 2005).

Havel, Vaclav, 'Politics, Morality and Civility', in Don E. Eberly (ed.), *The Essential Civil Society Reader: Classic Essays in the American Civil Society Debate* (New York: Rowman & Littlefield Publishers, 2000), pp. 391-402.

Hill, Lisa, 'The Hidden Theology of Adam Smith', *European Journal of the History of Economic Thought* 8.1 (2001), pp. 1-29.

Himmelfarb, Gertrude, 'The Renewal of Civil Society', in T. William Boxx and Gary M. (eds.), *Culture in Crisis and the Renewal of Civil Life* (Lanham, MD: Rowman and Littlefield Publishers, 1996), pp. 67-75.

Hodgson, Peter, *Winds of the Spirit: A Constructive Christian Theology* (Louisville, KY: Westminster/John Knox Press, 1994).

Holmes, Leslie, *Rotten States? Corruption, Post-Communism and Neoliberalism* (Durham and London: Duke University Press, 2006).

Hunt, Swanee, 'Raising Their Voices: Women in the New Democracies', *The Ambassadors Review*, Fall 1997 (the full text is at http://www.ksg.harvard.edu/wappp/happen/raising_voices.pdf).

Irenaeus, Saint, *Against Heresies*, book IV, ch. XIV, *The Apostolic Fathers with Justin Martyr and Irenaeus, Christian Classics Ethereal Library* (http://www.ccel.org/ccel/schaff/anf01.ix.vii.xv.html).

Johnson, Luke Thimothy, *The Literary Function of Possessions in Luke–Acts* (Missoula, MT: Scholars Press, 1977).

—*Sharing Possessions: Mandate and Symbol of Faith* (Philadelphia: Fortress Press, 1981).

—*The Acts of the Apostles* (Collegeville, MN: A Michael Glazier Book, The Liturgical Press, 1992).

Kant, Immanuel, *Idea for a Universal History from a Cosmopolitan Perspective* (1784) (full text at http://marxists.org/reference/subject/ethics/kant/universal-history.htm).

—*The Philosophy of History* (New York: Wiley Book Co. & Colonial Press, 1960).

—*Philosophy of Right* (trans. T.M. Knox; Oxford: The Clarendon Press, 1962).

—*Perpetual Peace: A Philosophical Essay* (trans. M. Campbell; New York & London: Grand Publishing, 1972)

Kärkkäinen, Veli-Matti, *An Introduction to Ecclesiology: Ecumenical, Historical & Global Perspectives* (Downers Grove, IL: InterVarsity Press, 2002).

Left, Carol Stalik, *The Czech and Slovak Republics: Nation Versus State* (Oxford: Westview Press, 1997).

Levinas, Emmanuel, *Totality and Infinity* (trans. Alphonso Lingis; Pittsburgh: Duquesne University Press, 1969).

—'The Ego and Totality', *Collected Philosophical Papers* (trans. Alphonso Lingis; Dordrecht, Netherlands: Martinus Hijhoff Publishers, 1987), pp. 25-48.

—*In the Time of the Nations* (trans. Michael B. Smith; London: The Atholone Press, 1994).

—*Beyond the Verse: Talmudic Readings and Lectures* (London: Continuum, 2007).

Lossky, Vladimir, *Orthodox Theology: An Introduction* (Crestwood, NY: St. Vladimir Seminary Press, 1978).

—*The Mystical Theology of the Eastern Church* (Crestwood, NY: St. Vladimir's Seminary Press, 1997).

Lloyd, David, 'Race under Representation', *Oxford Literary Review* 13.1-2 (1991), pp. 62-94.

Luxemburg, Rosa, 'Socialism and the Churches', *Marxist Classics* (http://www.newyouth.com/archives/clssics/luxemburg/socialismandthechurches.html).

Lyotard, J.-F., 'The Other's Rights', in S. Shute and S. Hurley (eds.), *On Human Rights* (New York: Basic Books, 1993), pp. 135-48.

Macchia, Frank, 'Tongues as a Sign: Towards a Sacramental Understanding of Tongues', *Pneuma* 15.1 (Spring 1993), pp. 61-76.

—*Baptized in the Spirit: A Global Pentecostal Theology* (Grand Rapids, MI: Zondervan, 2006).

Mann, Michael, *The Sources of Social Power* (2 vols; New York: Cambridge University Press, 1986).

Martinez, Samuel, 'Pentecostalism and Postcolonialism: Toward a Planetary Spiritual Network', paper presented at the 41st Annual Meeting of the Society for Pentecostal Studies, Regent University, Virginia Beach, Virginia, February 29-March 3, 2012.

Marx, Karl, *Critique of Hegel's 'Philosophy of Right'* (trans. Annette Jolin and Joseph O'Malley; Cambridge: Cambridge University Press, 1970).

Marx, Karl and Friedrich Engels, *The Communist Manifesto* (New York: Washington Squire Press, 1964).

McChesney, Robert W., 'Introduction', to Noam Chromsky, *Profit over People: Neoliberalism and Global Order* (New York: Steven Stories Press, 1999).

McFague, Sallie, 'An Ecological Christology: Does Christianity Have It?', in Dieter T. Hessel and Rosemary Redford Reuther (eds.), *Christianity and Ecology:*

Seeking the Well-Being of Earth and Humans (Cambridge, MA: Harvard University Press, 2000), pp. 29-45.

—*Life Abundant: Rethinking Theology an Economy for a Planet in Peril* (Minneapolis, MN: Augsburg Fortress, 2001).

—'Epilogue: The Human Dignity and the Integrity of Creation', in Darby Kathleen Ray (ed.), *Theology that Matters: Ecology, Economy and God* (Minneapolis: Fortress Press, 2006), pp. 199-212.

—*A New Climate for Theology: God, the World and Global Warming* (Minneapolis, MN: Fortress Press, 2008).

Meeks, M. Douglas, *God the Economist: The Doctrine of God and Political Economy* (Minneapolis, MN: Fortress Press, 1989).

Meyendorff, John, 'Doing Theology in an Eastern Orthodox Perspective', in Daniel B. Clendenin (ed.), *Eastern Orthodox Theology: A Contemporary Reader* (Grand Rapids, MI: Baker Books, 1995), pp. 79-96.

Mill, John Stuart, *On Liberty* (New York: Penguin Books, 1985).

Moltmann, Jürgen, *The Church in the Power of the Spirit* (Minneapolis, MN: Fortress Press, 1993).

—*The Trinity and the Kingdom* (Minneapolis, MN: Fortress Press, 1993).

—*Jesus Christ for Today's World* (Minneapolis, MN: Fortress Press, 1994).

Moore, Rickie D., '"They will know that a prophet has been among them": The Source and End of the Call of Ezekiel', in Steven J. Land, Rickie D. Moore, and John Christopher Thomas (eds.), *Passover, Pentecost and Parousia: Studies in Celebration of the Life and Ministry of R. Hollis Gause* (JPTSup 35; Blandford Forum: Deo Publishing, 2010), pp. 53-64.

Morgan, Maria Teresa, 'Tongues as of Fire: The Spirit as Paradigm for Ministry in a Multicultural Setting', in Bradford E. Hinze (ed.), *The Spirit in the Church and the World* (New York: Orbis Books, 2004), pp. 106-25.

Mount Jr., C. Eric, 'American Individualism Reconsidered', *Review of Religious Research* 22.4 (June 1981), 362-76.

Murove, Munyaradzi Felix, 'Perceptions of Greed in Western Economic and Religious Traditions: An African Communitarian Response', *Black Theology* 5.2 (2007), pp. 220-43.

Niebuhr, H. Richard, *Christ and Culture* (New York: Harper&Row Publishers, 1975).

Oliver O'Donovan, *Resurrection and Moral Order: An Outline for Evangelical Ethics* (Grand Rapids, MI: Eerdmans, 1994).

Olthuis, James H., ed. *Knowing Other-Wise: Philosophy at the Threshold of Spirituality* (New York: Fordham University Press, 1997)

Ouspensky, Leonid, *Theology of the Icon*, vol. 1 (Crestwood, NY: St. Vladimir's Seminary Press, 1992).

—'The Meaning of and Content of the Icon', in Daniel B. Clendenin (ed.), *Eastern Orthodox Theology* (Grand Rapids, MI: Baker Books, p. 1995), pp. 33-64.

Pfeil, Margaret R., 'Liturgy and Ethics: The Liturgical Asceticism of Energy Conservation', *Journal of the Society of Christian Ethics* 27.2 (Fall/Winter, 2007), pp. 127-49.

Pohl, Christine D., *Making Room: Recovering Hospitality as a Christian Tradition* (Grand Rapids, MI: Eerdmans, 1999).

Polanyi, Karl, *The Great Transformation: The Political and Economic Origins of Our Times* (New York: Farrar, Straus & Giroux, 1975).

Rad, Gerhard von, *Genesis* (trans. John H. Mark; Philadelphia: The Westminster Press, 1961).

Richter, Jan, 'Vaclav Klaus: The Experienced and Predictable', *Radio Prague*, Special Edition (February 7, 2008) transcript and audio at (http://www.radio.cz/en/section/election-special/vaclav-klaus-theexperience ed-and-predictable).

Ring, Sharon H., *Jesus, Liberation and the Biblical Jubilee: Images for Ethics and Christology* (Philadelphia: Fortress Press, 1985).

Rithart, Petr, 'Rival Visions: Vaclav Havel and Vaclav Klaus', *Journal of Democracy* 7.1 (1996), pp. 12-23.

Rosenblatt, Naomi H. and Joshua Horwitz, *Wrestling With Angels: What the First Family of Genesis Teaches Us About Our Spiritual Identity, Sexuality, and Personal Relationships* (New York: Delacorte Press, 1995).

Russel, Letty M., *Just Hospitality: God's Welcome in a World of Difference* (Louisville, KY: John Knox Press, 2009).

Schmemann, Alexander, *For the Life of the World* (Crestwood, NY: St Vladimir's Seminary Press, 1983).

—*Liturgy and Tradition* (ed. Thomas Fish; Crestwood, NY: St. Vladimir's Seminary Press, 1990).

—'The Missionary Imperative in the Orthodox Tradition', in Daniel B. Clendenin (ed.), *Eastern Orthodox Theology: A Contemporary Reader* (Grand Rapids, MI: Baker Books, 1995), pp. 195-210.

Sacks, Jonathan, *The Politics of Hope* (London: Vintage, 2000).

Soloviov, Vladimir, 'Троичное Начало и его Общественно Приложен ие', Чтения о Богочеловечество (Санкт-Петербург: Азбука, 2000).

Smith, Adam, *An Inquiry into the Nature and Causes of the Wealth of Nations* (London: William Benton Publisher, 1955).

—*The Theory of Moral Sentiments* (New York: Augustus M. Kelley Publishers, 1966).

Smith, James K.A., *Desiring the Kingdom: Worship, Worldview, and Cultural Formation* (Grand Rapids, MI: Baker Academic, 2009).

Stackhouse, Max, 'Sources and Prospects for Human Rights Ideas: A Christian Perspective', in Jindřich Halama (ed.), *The Idea of Human Rights: Traditions and Presence* (Prague, Czech Republic: UK ETF, 2003).

—'Public Theology and Political Economy in a Global Era', in William F. Storrar and Andrew R. Morton (eds.), *Public Theology for the 21st Century* (London: T&T Clark, 2004), pp. 179-94.

Staniloae, Dimitru, *The Experience of God: Orthodox Dogmatic Theology*, vol. 2 *The World: Creation and Deification* (Brookline, MA: Holy Cross Orthodox Press, 2005).

Stavropoulos, Christophoros, 'Partakers of Divine Nature', in Daniel B. Clendenin (ed.), *Eastern Orthodox Theology: A Contemporary Reader* (Grand Rapids, MI: Baker Books, 1995), pp. 183-92.

Steans, Jill, 'Globalization and Gender Inequality', in David Held and Anthony McGrew (eds.), *The Global Transformations Reader*, 2nd ed. (Oxford: Polity, 2003), pp. 455-63.

Stiglitz, Joseph E., *Globalization and its Discontents* (New York & London: W.W. Norton & Company, 2002).
Stroehlein, Andrew, 'Three Vaclavs', *Central Europe Review* 1.10 (30 August, 1999), pp. 1-4.
Stronstad, Rodger, *The Charismatic Theology of St. Luke* (Peabody, MA: Hendrickson Publishers, 1984).
—*The Prophethood of All Believers* (JPTSup 16; Sheffield: Sheffield Academic Press, 1999).
Tenner, Kathryn, *Theories of Culture: A New Agenda for Theology* (Minneapolis, MN: Fortress Press, 1997).
Thatcher, Margaret, Interview in the weekly periodical *Woman's Own*, London (July 1987).
Tiffany G. Petros, 'Mop, Shop and Shut up: Feminism in the Czech Republic', *Central Europe Review* 2.43 (11 December 2000): at (http://www.ce-review.org/00/43/petros43).
Toffler, Alvin, *Future Shock* (New York: Bantam Books, 1972).
Thomas, George, *Christian Ethics and Moral Philosophy* (New York: Scribners, 1955).
Thomas, John Christopher, *The Apocalypse: A Literary and Theological Commentary* (Cleveland, TN: CPT Press, 2012).
Thomas, Neill, *Makers of the Modern Mind* (Milwaukee: Bruce, 1949).
Tutu, Desmond, *The Rainbow People of God* (New York: Doubleday, 1994).
—*No Future without Forgiveness* (New York: Doubleday, 2000).
—*God Has a Dream: A Vision of Hope for Our Time* (New York: Doubleday, 2004).
Wanner, Catherine, *Communities of the Converted: Ukrainians and Global Evangelism* (Ithaca and London: Cornell University Press, 2007).
Williams, Wilbur Glenn, *Genesis: A Bible Commentary in the Wesleyan Tradition* (Indiana, IN: Wesleyan Publishing House, 2000).
Woolcock, Michael, 'Getting the Social Relations Right: Toward an Integrated Theology and Theory of Development', in Peter Heslam (ed.), *Globalization and the Good* (London: SPCK, 2004), pp. 41-51.
World Bank, *World Development Report 1996: From Plan to Market* (Oxford: Oxford University Press, 1996). (http://wdronline.worldbank.org//worldbank/a/c.html/world_development_report_1996/part_challenge_transition).
Wright, Ronald, *A Short History of Progress* (New York: Avalon, 2004).
Volf, Miroslav, *Exclusion and Embrace: A Theological Exploration of Identity, Otherness and Reconciliation* (Nashville: Abingdon Press, 1996).
—*After Our Likeness: The Church as the Image of the Trinity* (Grand Rapids, MI: Eerdmans, 1998).
Lucy Ward, 'After the Wall', *Guardian* (Thursday, 23 September, 1999), at (http://www.guardian.co.uk/print/0,3858,3904787-103691,00.html).
Ware, Timothy (Bishop Kallisos), *The Orthodox Church* (New York: Penguin Books, 1997).
Warrington, Keith, *Pentecostal Theology: A Theology of Encounter* (London: T & T Clark, 2008).
Weber, Max, *The Protestant Ethic and the 'Spirit' of Capitalism* (New York: The Penguin Group, 2002).

Wenk, Matthias, *Community-Forming Power: The Socio-Ethical Role of the Spirit in Luke–Acts* (JPTSup 19; Sheffield: Sheffield Academic Press, 2000).

Wright, Robin, 'The New Tribalism: Defending Human Rights in the Age of Ethnic Conflict', *Los Angelis Times*, June 08, 1993.

Wyschogrod, Edith, *Saints and Postmodernity: Revisioning Moral Philosophy* (Chicago: University of Chicago Press, 1990).

Yegenoglou, Mayda, 'Liberal Multiculturalism and the Ethics of Hospitality in the Age of Globalization', *Postmodern Culture* (http://www3.iath.virginia.edu/pmc/issue.103/13.2yegenoglu.html).

Yong, Amos, *Hospitality and the Other: Pentecost, Christian Practices, and the Neighbor* (Maryknoll, NY: Orbis Books, 2008).

Zizek, Slavoj, 'Multiculturalism, Or, the Cultural Logic of Multinational Capitalism', I/225 *New Left Review* (September/October 1997), pp. 28-51.

Zappen, James P., 'Mikhail Bakhtin', in Michael G. Morgan and Michelle Ballif (eds.), *Twentieth-Century Rhetoric and Rhetoricians: Critical Studies and Sources* (Westport: Greenwood Press, 2000), pp. 7-20.

Zizioulas, John D., *Being as Communion: Studies in Personhood and the Church* (Crestwood, NY: St. Vladimir's Seminary Press, 1995).

Index of Biblical References

Index of Names

54504207R00098

Made in the USA
Columbia, SC
01 April 2019